# ADVANCE PRAISE

## *RECONSIDERING JANE JACOBS*

"'Please look closely at real cities,' Jane Jacobs wrote 50 years ago on the first page of *The Death and Life of Great American Cities*—and what has been the consequence? The 12 compelling essays in *Reconsidering Jane Jacobs* faithfully record both the tremendous and continuing impacts that Jane Jacobs's own observations have had on the world, and the dissatisfactions and difficulties many still have with her way of observing and learning about cities—'listen, linger and think about what you see' were her instructions. This is a fascinating, complex, and honest book."

> —Tony Hiss | author of *In Motion* and *The Experience of Place*;
> visiting scholar at New York University's Robert F. Wagner
> Graduate School of Public Service

"Nothing demonstrates the need for this book more vividly than Max Page's opening story of viewing Jane Jacobs's 'utterly ordinary' West Village home, a narrow three-story building on Hudson Street where she lived in the 1950s and '60s, on sale in 2009 for $3.5 million. The hyper-gentrification of Lower Manhattan is just one symptom of the complicated legacy left by Jacobs, revered goddess of urban theory. The essays in this expansive collection interrogate and excavate the real details of Jacobs's thought. It will clarify and deepen Jacobs's ideas for novices and aficionados alike."

> —Mark Kingwell | professor of philosophy, University of Toronto,
> author of *Concrete Reveries: Consciousness and the City*

# RECONSIDERING
# JANE JACOBS

# Reconsidering Jane Jacobs

Edited by

Max Page and Timothy Mennel

American Planning Association
**Planners Press**

*Making Great Communities Happen*

**Chicago | Washington, D.C.**

Copyright © 2011 by the American Planning Association

205 N. Michigan Ave., Suite 1200, Chicago, IL 60601-5927

1030 15th St., NW, Suite 750 West, Washington, DC 20005-1503

www.planning.org/plannerspress

ISBN: 978-1-932364-94-1 (cloth)

978-1-932364-95-8 (pbk.)

Library of Congress Control Number 2010919602

Printed in the United States of America

10 9 8 7 6 5 4 3 2 1

# CONTENTS

# RECONSIDERING
# JANE JACOBS

# INTRODUCTION:

## MORE THAN MEETS THE EYE

I followed the trail of a real estate advertisement. The three-story building at 555 Hudson Street, where Jane Jacobs lived in the 1950s and 1960s, was for sale in 2009 for a cool $3.5 million. I went expecting some kind of spiritual connection to the great urbanist, as if, 40 years after she left the house, nothing would have changed. But I also went to look from her windows, to see what she had seen. I had high expectations, which were met, not surprisingly, by a high level of disappointment. It was nothing more than a decent, somewhat rickety, narrow house in a very good location with a first-floor retail space, an open living room and small kitchen on the second floor, tiny bedrooms on the third floor, a dark backyard (with a fence memorably captured by Diane Arbus when she photographed Jane Jacobs and her son Ned), a lovely third-floor patio. Temporary furniture placed by the real estate company to help sell the house was still there, awaiting the new owners' design choices.

The utter ordinariness of that house and the utterly insane price it went for—average for the neighborhood—say a lot about Jane Jacobs and about the purposes of this volume of essays.

This book emerged out of a belief that there are contradictions in Jane Jacobs's thought and influence that deserve further discussion. This might seem like an odd statement. Over the years, as Richard Harris describes here through a close look at citation indexes, Jane Jacobs has been written about thousands of times. And since her death, there have been exhibits, biographies, panels, and even annual "Jane's Walks" in cities around the world. Is there any American architect, planner, or preservationist over the age of 30 who has not read her or could not at least reel off the outline of *The Death and*

*Life of Great American Cities*? Is there any other writer on cities in the United States whose works are still so widely read?

Because the answer to these questions is "no," we suggest two more questions: Is there any other urbanist whose ideas more people profess to understand who is less understood? And is there another urbanist whose influence is so widely felt even where her name is not well known? We suggest in this volume that the answer is again "no": Many who profess to understand Jacobs's ideas don't, and many more who profess not to know of her work have in fact been deeply influenced by it. Like Freud's, her ideas are everywhere, named or unnamed.

And to use Freudian terminology, many have found her to be a beckoning screen on which to project their ideologies. Jane Jacobs has had lasting power for many reasons, but one of them certainly is that she offers something for everyone. As Francis Morrone has noted, Jane Jacobs has drawn the praise of new urbanists and preservationists, free-market capitalists, and advocates of government regulation.[1] She is a right-wing libertarian, and she is a left-wing antiwar protester. She cherishes the small-business owner and rails against bureaucrats who limit innovation, and she is also the symbol of one of the things conservatives in the 2008 presidential election scoffed at: "the community activist." Her writing is remarkably accessible to the average reader and seems open to all political viewpoints. As Gert-Jan Hospers, one of our contributors, writes, she "did not like ideologies at all." But many ideologies, and ideologues, have found themselves and their ideas in her pages, spawning a celebration of Jane Jacobs across the political spectrum.

This volume also came about in part out of a frustration with this near beatification of Jane Jacobs. Despite the passing of nearly five decades since the publication of *Death and Life* (1961), the image of "Saint Jane" persists.[2] She is treated as infallible and unquestionable. For far too many in the urban planning world, the bracelets that say "WWJD" (What Would Jesus Do?) may as well stand for What Would Jane Do? Would she approve of this or that project? people ask. Does it have all the elements she required?

This volume, however, is not intended as hero-toppling revisionism. It is, as the title indicates, a reconsideration of Jane Jacobs. We offer in some ways the highest level of respect for Jane Jacobs because we aim to take her seriously, as a profoundly important figure, and not a stick figure. In recruiting contributors, we sought out people who would look at the range of her thinking and evaluate her greatest contributions but also wrestle with her blind spots, her contradictory political impulses. We also wanted to look at the unintended uses to which her writing has been put. This volume is less about Jane Jacobs as an individual than about "Jane Jacobs" as the shorthand for a set of ideas and planning practices that have spread around the world over the past half century, some of which the individual named Jane Jacobs might not have recognized as her own.

We think it is valuable, for example, to highlight—as Jamin Creed Rowan and Peter L. Laurence do—that Jane Jacobs was of her time, a product and follower of urban renewal ideas who then rejected that approach to city building. To say that there were many others—such as J. B. Jackson and Herbert Gans—who were challenging the precepts of modernism and urban renewal in the 1950s does nothing to undermine the importance of Jane Jacobs's thought and her particular ability to explain the workings of seemingly incomprehensible cities. Virtually every author and professor who has spoken about Jane Jacobs has commented on her brilliant writing technique, but hardly any have placed her within the writing traditions of her time, as Jamin Creed Rowan does. A close look at Jacobs's rhetorical techniques reminds us of the declension of architectural writing in the half century since *Death and Life*, especially that coming out of architecture schools. Architecture students who are flummoxed by virtually all of what passes for architectural theory today find themselves empowered by reading Jane Jacobs. Is there any other nonfiction writer about cities whom one can read out loud, paragraph after paragraph, to one's students and have them enthralled?

We think it worthwhile to look more closely at the connection between Jane Jacobs and the most important planning movement to emerge in the last decades of the 20th century, new urbanism. Jill L. Grant explores the works of the key theorists and practitioners of new urbanism and finds a deep but selective use of Jacobs's ideas. Like those developers that preserve the façade of a historic structure and build a glass tower behind, new urbanists adopted Jacobs's easy-to-master ideas about urban design but stripped them of their place within a rich argument about the value of complexity, the necessity of inefficiency, and the value of public space and government action.

And we find it vitally important to begin the process of understanding the influence of her ideas around the world. Interspersed between the longer essays are shorter reports from around the world, including Abu Dhabi, the Netherlands, China, Argentina, and Australia. Their stories may be surprising to readers. While her reception in Europe was generally smoother than in her home country, the adoption of her ideas varied widely. In some places, such as Argentina, where a Spanish translation of one of her works lay deep in the stacks of the one library that owned it, Jane Jacobs is only now getting a following, as a nascent preservation movement in creatively destructive Buenos Aires seeks a philosophical grounding. The "other" Jane Jacobs—urban geographer Jane M. Jacobs—finds that Jane Jacobs was hardly central to the thinking of planners in Australia in the 1960s and 1970s. Planning remained, she writes, much more linked to the traditions of Great Britain, a slow-dying legacy of the empire. But in all these places, we are reminded that Jane Jacobs remains, 50 years after *Death and Life*, an important figure whose influence continues to evolve.

## 555

As I write these lines, I am looking out over the poet Emily Dickinson's grave, which I can see from my house. Two blocks to the south is the Dickinson Homestead, where she was born and famously lived in near seclusion from the wider world most of her life. She attended Amherst Academy, a few hundred yards to the west. She built new worlds out of the sparest number of words but rarely left a few hundred square yards. There has never been a writer more closely tied to a town and even a single house and surrounding landscape than Emily Dickinson.

And there never has been an urbanist who influenced so many around the world who has been more identified—however incompletely—with the home and neighborhood where she began writing about cities than Jane Jacobs.

For although Jacobs read widely and observed with an incisive eye the urban decay, government blunders, and architectural inanities that had spread like a cancer over urban areas by the late 1950s, her theories of city design and development were crafted by an engagement with the world immediately around her: a few blocks on and around Hudson Street in New York's Greenwich Village. It was from her observations of street life and economic activity—often from the windows of her narrow town house—that Jacobs crystallized her belief in the centrality of economic diversity to healthy cities and isolated the sources of urban social and cultural dynamism, which were not hidden but in fact right before all of our eyes. Even though the specific references in her work to her neighborhood represent only a small part of *Death and Life* or any of her other works, it is these accounts—of a day in the life of this neighborhood, of the "street ballet" she participated in daily—that continue to resonate 50 years later. Indeed, it is the witty common sense—which formed the basis of a much larger three-volume theory of cities, as Richard Harris argues in this book—gleaned from everyday life that makes the book so memorable and that is a large part of its lasting influence.

Like virtually every student or practitioner of architecture, urban planning, and urban studies over the past 50 years in the United States, I was reared on Jane Jacobs—on *Death and Life* primarily and on *The Economy of Cities* and *Cities and the Wealth of Nations*.[3] I used to live a few blocks from the intersection of Hudson and Perry Streets and would occasionally walk by, almost as if on a pilgrimage. But in 2009 when I went back to that most famous of houses in the history of American urban planning, I went not to gawk from the outside but to get inside.

The view from the second-floor living room of 555 Hudson Street was nothing remarkable: people passing every few seconds, an apartment building across the street, cars in rhythmic movement northward, the indeterminate sounds of the city. Ordinary city life.

This was, of course, Jacobs's genius: to look out on a typical street and see not dirt, traffic, and the old in need of updating but rather something akin to a utopia of the ordinary. It was, as Robert Venturi, clearly influenced by *Death and Life*, later wrote, "ugly and ordinary," and it was "almost alright."[4] But Jane Jacobs thought it was more than "alright." What she believed in and argued for, over the course of three volumes, was a new theory of economic growth that was rooted in diverse, dense, efficiently inefficient cities, where new work was added to old work to make the wealth of nations.

Though Thomas Kuhn's phrase *paradigm shift* is often overused, it is a notion that applies well here.[5] City planning strategies that had come to be accepted—even by Jacobs, as Peter L. Laurence argues in this volume—were rapidly upended once their essential mistakes were laid bare, not slowly and steadily but rapidly and radically, with Jane Jacobs leading the campaign.

Planners of the day believed that the aerial view of the city was liberating, giving inspiration to the progressive and the modern. The airplane had made it possible to grasp the entire city and then plan rationally for its future. The dream of the planner was to act as did the creators of Futurama at the World's Fair in 1939—picking up pieces of the future city, moving towers here and there, laying down highways through the old city in the most "efficient" manner. That was one version of planning for the modern city.

Jane Jacobs dismantled this theory of planning with word-swords that left it mortally wounded for two generations. By looking out the windows of her three-story house on Hudson Street and studying closely the life of her street, she proved that the aerial view was flawed and led toward destructive ends. After neighborhoods had been demolished and the highway, wide-open plaza, or housing project had been built, the result was, as Walter Benjamin said about his sorted library bookshelves, "the mild boredom of order."[6] It was the view of the street that was rich, mind opening, and complex. Her neighborhood, typically brushed aside with a wave of the hand as being disorganized, inefficient, and economically backward, was in fact a place of "organized complexity"—a seemingly chaotic human ecosystem that, if truly understood, was as ordered and economically efficient and robust as any place. Indeed, it was far more viable and vibrant than neighborhoods built from plans made from aerial views. It was the view of the street—the veins of the metropolis's body—that was liberating and expansive. Here was an alternative view of modernism.

Even as my admiration for Jane Jacobs soared as I newly appreciated her ability to see what others had ignored, that $3.5 million price tag gnawed. Jane Jacobs fought alongside others in the early 1960s to save the West Village from destruction and won an important victory that would ultimately bring down the urban renewal edifice. But while she saved the neighborhood, she did not foresee what it might become—an area nearly uniformly for the wealthy. On the outside, everything has been preserved—a remarkable victory against yet another urban renewal project. But behind the façades, the neighborhood has been utterly transformed by a postindustrial, post-Fordist, globalized economy that has re-sorted New York, clearing Manhattan of the working classes in order to make way for those at the top of the new Gilded Age. Without intending to, and perhaps without being able to see clearly enough into the future, she made the neighborhood safe for $3.5 million town houses.

This book will no doubt be seen in light of a larger reconsideration of the dominant narrative of planning over the past generation. Jane Jacobs and her reputed shadow figure Robert Moses—whom she in reality confronted only rarely; they were like jousters on parallel tracks—have come to define, in the hands of city narrators eager for a simple way to encapsulate the complex story of postwar New York, two fundamentally different approaches to city building.[7]

Robert Moses's image was set in the three-pound paper rock that is Robert Caro's brilliant *The Power Broker* in 1974. A whole generation of architects, planners, and other city people were educated to despise Moses and all that he represented. (It was hard to find a defender, and hardly a word in his favor, at Yale, where I first wrestled with the ideas of both Moses and Jacobs as an undergraduate in the 1980s.) The opposite was Jane Jacobs, who was a writer as good as Caro and who represented—or came to represent for those who wanted to easily summarize and simplify her ideas—a wholly different idea of city building.

But that has begun to change. As Caro came out with his multivolume series on Lyndon Johnson and readers noted that the theme of that story was remarkably similar to the theme of *The Power Broker*—brilliant, idealistic leader corrupted by power—they wondered if in fact Moses had been subjected to historical typecasting and in critical ways misrepresented. More important, frustration with the inability of American planners and architects to get major public and private projects completed led many to question whether the community planning structures and ethos that Jane Jacobs had inspired were really best for New York or other cities. Frustration grew as megacities expanded across Latin America, Africa, and especially East Asia, and governments remade those cities rapidly and, in some aspects, beautifully. A new look at old truisms was in order. In 2007, a series of exhibitions and the publication of a large volume looking at Robert Moses in New York gave Moses due respect for the full range of his projects, from small parks and large public pools to the better-known highways and bridges and urban renewal projects. The exhibitions, book, and related events brought out into the open a hushed debate that had gone on among planners, architects, and historians for many years.[8]

In this volume, both Thomas J. Campanella and Nathan Cherry won-der—as have others, such as Samuel Zipp in his recent book on postwar New York—whether we have lost the "collective public commitment" that urban renewal, at its best, represented.[9] While Cherry and Campanella each cite China's ability to pull off large-scale projects with dispatch, they readily acknowledge the danger of romanticizing China's authoritarian approach to planning and politics. But they leave us thinking about what we might have lost in the rejection of the urban renewal ethos. Cam-panella, who spent several years in Beijing writing about the explosive growth of China's cities, further reflects on Jane Jacobs's questionable influence on planning. In launching, as she wrote on the opening page of *Death and Life*, "an attack on current city planning and rebuilding," Jacobs also achieved the diminution of the planning profession's identity as a unique field with appropriate authority in public debates.[10] Worst of all, according to Campanella, in the wake of Jacobs's attacks planning also lost much of its visionary capacity. The failure to respond to the recent, and worst, recession since the Great Depression with a robust reinvestment in infrastructure, as happened in the 1930s, was tragically typical of the nation's foreshortened horizons. The United States missed the opportunity to rebuild in a way that would allow it to thrive in the new century, and one has to wonder if one author of this timidity was the sage of Hudson Street.

## 225

Jane Jacobs gave Gotham one of its highest compliments by dedicating *Death and Life* "To New York City, where I came to seek my fortune."[11] In *Systems of Survival* (1992), she was a little more specific, thanking her three primary homes in Scranton, Pennsylvania; New York; and Toronto: "To 1712 Monroe Avenue, 555 Hudson Street, and 69 Albany Avenue."[12] She might as well have also thanked 225 West 4th Street in Greenwich Vil-lage, a few short blocks from her home on Hudson Street, where, as Jamin Creed Rowan tells us, she rented a studio to write *Death and Life*. This is hardly an anonymous location, right at the intersection of 7th Avenue, oth-erwise known as Sheridan Square. Christopher Street crosses here; at 53 Christopher, around the corner from Jacobs's writing studio, is the location of the Stonewall Inn. That bar, which became the site of the infamous riot in 1969, opened just before Jane Jacobs left for Canada. But even when she was working there, the neighborhood had already become an important gathering area for the gay community.

In other words, Jane Jacobs crafted her theory of city development at what might be considered the ground zero of the cultural revolutions of the 1950s and 1960s. But you would never know it.

Greenwich Village, where Jane Jacobs lived and learned about the value of urban life, was arguably the center of the cultural avant-garde of the United States in the 1950s and 1960s, where new forms of art, dance, and literature were pioneered and where the feminist and gay rights movements found a home and grew. But even though she lived there, Jane Jacobs hardly mentions how the character of cultural production and cultural interaction was aided by the form of the neighborhood. One could read *Death and Life*—and *Economy of Cities* and *Cities and Wealth*—and never know the Beats existed or that just blocks from her home on Hudson Street and outside the window of her writing studio were some of the most vibrant settings for theater, music, and art, as well as more informal settings of cultural and social innovation.

While Jane Jacobs has often been credited with celebrating the flux of the big city, it is not the heart of the big city and its vibrant cultural and social movements that she portrayed in *Death and Life* but rather a quiet section that seemed to remain out of the reach of the most powerful forces in the city. Marshall Berman long ago argued that Jacobs is so important because she embraced the city as a place of rapid and radical change. She showed, he has written, that "the meaning for which modern men and women were searching lay surprisingly close to home, in the perpetual motion and change of the city, and evanescent but intense and complex face-to-face communication and communion."[13] I always had my doubts: The "modernism of the streets" that Berman so cherished was a far cry from the city of daily repetition and friendly interactions in Jacobs's world. And Berman began to wonder as well. Two decades after writing this paean to Jacobs, Berman wrote that when it appeared, "Jacobs's vision seemed so direct and straightforward," but "today, we've got to wonder, is this pragmatism or pastoral? Is it direct experience of city life or a grid of prescribed happy meanings forcibly imposed on city life?"[14] The great city is a place not of repetition of daily tasks and interactions but of startling change and confusion, and also stunning cultural and social innovation. It is a great paradox that the city's vitality comes not from the rather staid interactions of a backwater neighborhood but from the chaotic and destructive arenas of social, political, economic, and cultural interaction.

While Jacobs's vision was a powerful one—and a convincing antidote to urban renewal policies of the 1950s—it was a vision laced with nostalgia. Unfortunately, it is to this nostalgia that developers have responded in the past two decades. They have simplified and bundled together various invented traditions of the bustling small town, building whole, instantaneous developments that mimic in stilted ways the principles of community development laid out by Jane Jacobs. Typical developments such as "Main Street" in Voorhees, New Jersey, and Kentlands in Gaithersburg, Maryland, have most of the features Jacobs discusses in *Death and Life*—short blocks, a mixture of housing and business, relatively high density. But one glance at the fake parking meters, the exclusive boutiques, and the expensive condominiums above them makes it obvious that these developments are pathetic mockeries of real cities. ("Main Street" has since gone bankrupt, something Jacobs no doubt would have predicted.) And malls and big box stores throughout the United States have, in the process of sapping the life from downtown business districts, copied the Victorian-era business fronts and tried to recreate small-town morphology under a big roof, with extensive parking on all sides. Not unlike Frank Lloyd Wright, whose Prairie style spawned copycat suburban tract houses and the homogeneous suburbs he detested, Jane Jacobs, in her unwillingness to confront the dynamism of the city, smoothed the way for the suburban and exurban excesses of today.

This radical transformation of our cities—into suburban and exurban metropolitan areas, gated communities, racially and economically segregated urban centers—threatens to undermine the physical network of spaces that is essential to the exercise of democratic life and values. "Democracy is in the streets" went the slogan from the 1960s. But it is as true as Students for a Democratic Society protestors thought: Our democracy has been built around sites of public discussion and protest, streets and sidewalks, town commons and town squares—all public and available to be used and appropriated to make a point. In a privatized urban landscape—some 40 million Americans live in wholly private and gated communities, and most of us shop in malls and Walmarts where there are no free speech rights—confrontation with diverging political ideas and agendas is merely optional.

In order to stem this transformation, an alternative story of the cultural life of cities needs to be told and an alternative urbanism imagined.

## 192

In the middle of graduate school, when I returned to New York to live and conduct research for my dissertation, I moved into an apartment at 192 Sixth Avenue in Soho, a short walk from 555 Hudson Street. I bragged to my friends that I lived in a "real Jane Jacobs neighborhood." I sat on my stoop, watched parents play with children in a tiny park, and shook my head at the huge apartment building across the street, which had surely decimated nice old stoops like the one I was sitting on. I noted with smugness that all the stores in the basement floors of my tenement row were doing well and that the mirror ones across the street, beneath the 12-story apartment building, were virtually all empty. People mentioned that cars were more likely to be broken into over there because there were no "eyes on the street."

But even as I celebrated my little corner of New York, I realized that it was not this small place that defined New York for me. Rather, I found the character of the city in the contrast between the relative stability and familiarity of this neighborhood and the overheated bustle of other parts of the city, symbolized by the trucks and cabs that flew by on Sixth Avenue and the packed multitudes who rumbled by on the A train beneath the street. The sense of place of the city emanates not from stability, stasis, repetition, and homogeneity but from convulsive change, which is often destructive but also historically and potentially creative.

I continue to wish that rather than moving out from the microscopic to the global and more theoretical, as she did in her later works, Jane Jacobs—still our greatest, most eloquent defender of urban life—had instead moved through the city to explain in her unmatched style the different dynamics, the different "ballets" of the city. Perhaps if she had continued, over the years and through her books, to focus on the experience of the city, she may have been able to provide us with the eloquent, passionate defense of the city that we need: one that truly embraces the city's social and cultural interactions, fusions, and conflicts. The Mexican author Carlos Fuentes has written that "people and their cultures perish in isolation, but they are born or reborn in contact with other men and women."[15] It is in the city that this contact and this rebirth happen. It is only by recognizing and valuing this central idea of city life that we can fully embrace the notion of the city as a place for dreaming of new forms of human relations, new cultural developments, and new social and political arrangements.

But the starting point has to be observation so close and sustained that it cultivates an instinct for what works in a particular place—a quality that Bill Bradley, as a young basketball star, described to John McPhee as "a sense of where you are."[16] And for this, we have no better guide and prophet than Jane Jacobs. Before the famous opening lines of *Death and Life*, Jacobs included a page entitled "Illustrations." There are, of course, no illustrations in the book. But Jacobs had a point to make: "The scenes that illustrate this book are all about us. For illustrations, please look closely at real cities. While you are looking, you might as well also listen, linger and think about what you see."[17]

# THE UNKNOWN JANE JACOBS:
## GEOGRAPHER, PROPAGANDIST,
## CITY PLANNING IDEALIST

### PETER L. LAURENCE

In great contrast to the emblem of anti-planning that she became, there was a time when Jane Jacobs idealized the field of city planning and supported urban renewal. This was in the early 1950s, and she was in good company then. The field was relatively young and full of promise, and urban redevelopment and renewal policies were broadly supported, the federal urban redevelopment and renewal Housing Acts of 1949 and 1954 being fundamentally bipartisan. But Jacobs, perhaps more than most, embraced the idea of city planning with all the commitment of an enthusiast, imagining it as a model intellectual practice—one in which decisions were based not on abstractions and assumptions about city life but on direct study of the city through a research-oriented approach. City planning was then nearly identical to the field and practice that, in her later disillusionment, Jacobs would reinvent in *The Death and Life of Great American Cities*.

With *Death and Life*, Jacobs dealt an epic blow to a multibillion-dollar regime of federal and local policies, agencies, and real estate development interests; articulated the bankruptcy of prevailing city planning theories; and wrote one of the most important books on cities and city life. And she achieved what she set out to achieve: to present a "new system of thought about the great city"—the foundation for an idealized field of city planning, architecture, and urban design that would recognize the complexity and fragile intricacy of the great city.[1] It is a system of thought that we have all embraced.

Despite her great achievements, Jacobs was not exactly the embodiment of Olympian urban wisdom that 50 years of commentary have invented, however. She was much greater than the lingering stereotypes of 1950s America that still have her pegged as an amateur and a housewife who could comprehend no more than the domestic simplicity of Greenwich Village. She was in fact educated in geography and economic geography, fields to which she later significantly contributed. A professional with a lifetime career as a writer, she was already among the most important writers on the city before *Death and Life* was published. But she was less than the mythological saint of the city whose mantra has become "WWJJD?" (What Would Jane Jacobs Do?) That Jacobs, our own idealization, will inevitably disappoint us, as the idealized city planner once disappointed her. However, as Jacobs knew well from experience, that sort of sycophantism is escapism from the daily labor of building knowledge and cities here and now, through our own work, ourselves.

## JANE JACOBS: URBAN GEOGRAPHER

We would think of Jacobs differently had she completed her studies at Columbia University in the early 1940s. Many of her books would likely be shelved with those in geography, particularly economic geography (fields in which she trained), and not in the sociology section (a field in which she took only one course, which she did not like), as the back cover of *Death and Life* suggests. With a degree in hand, she might have even become an academic under the right circumstances, in which case she would probably have continued to write, although we might not be reading her work today.

Such speculation aside, when Jacobs decided to go to college in the late 1930s and enrolled in Columbia's University Extension program (later renamed the School of General Studies), she took courses in a variety of subjects—including philosophy, patent law, constitutional law, and the development of legal institutions—but most of her course work was in geography. The courses in philosophy, constitutional law, and legal institutions inspired her first—and little-known—book, *Constitutional Chaff: Rejected Suggestions of the Constitutional Convention of 1787* (1941), a study published by Columbia University Press under her maiden name. It might have been a nice start for an academic: It received a brief but favorable review by the eminent constitutional scholar Max Farrand in the *American Historical Review* and is still cited in scholarly papers today by those who may not know that Jane Butzner was also Jane Jacobs. Much later, it appears that this early work was motivated by the same questions as *Systems of Survival: A Dialogue on the Moral Foundations of Commerce and Politics* (1992), which was equally concerned with understanding underlying cultural structures and their possibilities. However, *The Death and Life of Great American Cities* (1961), *The Economy of Cities* (1969), *Cities and the Wealth of Nations* (1984), and *The Nature of Economies* (2000), one of her last and greatest books, were all informed by her early studies in geography and economic geography.

In the late 1930s, economic geography, a relatively young field, was an important part of Columbia University's large Department of Geography, whose multidisciplinary approach appealed to Jacobs. At Columbia, geography was understood to involve "at least two fields of learning—physiography and one other such as economics, history, botany, zoology"—with students developing a specialization within the field. At higher levels of study, the program was administered by a multidisciplinary committee—including a professor of physiography, a professor of economic geography, and other appropriate disciplinary representatives—instead of being "in the hands of any one school or department of the university."[2] This reflected the idea that while geography was considered the "Mother of the Sciences," it was distinct from the physical geography studied in departments of geology. As defined by the president of the Association of American Geographers in 1922, geography was "the science of *human ecology*," a study that emphasized the reciprocities between human activity and the environment.[3] This was a theme that Jacobs had already explored in her first essays on the city, published in *Vogue*, and it would be a central principle in her lifework.

Among the faculty under whom Jacobs studied was economic geography professor Herman Otte. He specialized in the economics of the Tennessee Valley Authority (TVA), the multistate regional planning agency created by President Roosevelt in 1933, which Jacobs later discussed at length in *Cities and the Wealth of Nations*.[4] There she critiqued the idea that a region could become significantly productive without the economic and cultural development stimulated by a great city. Despite the contemporary assumption that she necessarily supported FDR's New Deal because she was a liberal, the TVA was the sort of federal project that Jacobs already opposed in the 1930s and was among the reasons why she enthusiastically supported anyone who was running against FDR.

Among the most significant influences on her at Columbia was Jacobs's discovery—perhaps in Otte's economic geography courses—of Henri Pirenne's *Medieval Cities: Their Origins and the Revival of Trade* (1925), one of the single most influential books on her thinking about cities. In her last book, *Dark Age Ahead* (2004), she wrote that Pirenne "laid the foundations for modern understanding of cities" and that *Medieval Cities* was "a basic text for understanding how the world's economic networks operate and how they fail."[5] While confirming her esteem for Pirenne's ideas, the acknowledgment actually underemphasized the inestimable influence of his book on her own study of cities, economies, and civilization. Jacobs not only cited Pirenne in most of her books but also drew major themes from *Medieval Cities* and expanded on them in *The Economy of Cities*, *Cities and the Wealth of Nations*, and *Systems of Survival*.[6] In *The Economy of Cities*, Jacobs drew heavily on Pirenne's research on the origins of European cities to explain how cities grew and how they failed. In *Cities and the Wealth of Nations*, she was influenced by his history of the development of cities into great cities and into city-states that were nations unto themselves. In *Systems of Survival*, Jacobs was particularly influenced by Pirenne's discussion of the tensions between economic and political organization, and the way that economic transformations in the 11th century simultaneously gave rise to cities and the social change that freed serfs from agricultural servitude, created a powerful and productive middle class (the term was Pirenne's), and prompted unprecedented structures of liberty and democracy, namely, civilization. In *Systems of Survival*, Jacobs expanded on the theme of "Traders vs. Guardians," her shorthand for the often competing syndromes of commerce (freedom of economic and cultural exchange) and authority (control of economic and cultural exchange) to which Pirenne alluded.

It is clear, moreover, that Pirenne's book was on Jacobs's mind when she set out to write *Death and Life*. Pirenne not only outlined the qualities of a great city; *Medieval Cities* was, above all, an explanation of the "death and life" of cities after the collapse of the Roman Empire (a theme Jacobs also discussed in *Dark Age Ahead*) and the reemergence of cities following the revival of exchange and urban economies. *Medieval Cities* was especially timely in the 1950s, when cities were threatened from within and without by suburban and antiurban forces and the influence of the middle class, which, as Pirenne had explained, was historically important to the city's prosperity. Thus, when she first outlined her book proposal for *Death and Life* in 1958, Jacobs offered that Pirenne's work had "much to say on how life is organized in contemporary cities."[7]

In the big picture, however, for Jacobs the significance of geography was its powerful and synthetic interdisciplinarity. In geography, her studies in biology, zoology, geology, and economic geography, rather than being random or unrelated interests, as presumed by previous commentators, all fell within the context of a larger field of study. For her, the study of natural ecology complemented and informed the study of human ecology in Columbia's "two fields of study" model. The related interests in the natural and life sciences that Jacobs cultivated at Columbia synthesized with her studies in geography to produce seminal theories of city functions and dynamics; the life sciences were her key to developing and transcending Pirenne's historically oriented theories of the death and life of cities to form new and timeless principles about city dynamics. So although Jacobs wrote in the introduction to the 1993 Modern Library edition of *Death and Life* that, in the course of writing the book, she realized she was "engaged in studying the ecology of cities," there is evidence that her study had in fact started much earlier.[8] Indeed, when Jacobs left Columbia in 1940, she had already begun to think of herself as a "city naturalist."[9]

## JANE JACOBS: PROFESSIONAL WRITER

Jacobs left Columbia before graduating, with a bitterness toward academe that would remain with her throughout her life. Without a college degree, she was irrevocably set on the career path of becoming a professional writer. It was a project that she pursued with characteristic determination and initiative.

Leaving the oasis of the Columbia campus for the streets of New York, to immerse herself once again in what she described in *Systems of Survival* as "the great world of work," must have been a moment of déjà vu.[10] Jacobs hadn't gone to college following high school in order to learn "how the world works" firsthand and to pursue a career as a writer; now she was out of the academy and in the city again.[11] The anecdote that she told decades later, when interest first emerged in her biography with the publication of *Death and Life*, was that she was effectively expelled for having earned too many credits for an extension program student. Having pursued a full-time student load and earned 65 credits in two years in the same courses full-time majors enrolled in, she was forced to apply to Barnard Women's College, which did not admit her, ostensibly because of her poor high school grades. She famously quipped in a rare autobiographical exposition that the rejection allowed her "to continue getting an education."[12] Jacobs was genuinely embittered enough to reject honorary degrees decades later and to write scathingly about higher education as a credentialing operation in her last book-cum-memoir, *Dark Age Ahead*, and the anecdote has been repeated often enough to obscure the good memories and formative experiences that Jacobs had in her two years as a college student.

After finishing the manuscript for *Constitutional Chaff*, Jacobs might have taken almost any full-time job to support herself and develop her writing career—and she took a position as secretary to the managing editor of *Iron Age*, a weekly trade magazine for the metals industry published by the Chilton Company. Jacobs already had some practical experience of the metals industry that she could build on, from her earliest part-time work in New York at Peter Frasse and Company steelworks, as well as some basic knowledge of geology and chemistry from her courses at Columbia, and given her intellectual interest in the world of work, *Iron Age* appealed to her beyond the day-to-day responsibilities—at least initially. The magazine offered a bird's-eye view of an elemental part of the national and regional economy, providing an opportunity to extend her interests in economic geography into the real world. Moreover, for a philosophically minded writer, practical experiences in the world of work always had a contemplative component. As in *Death and Life* and her subsequent books, experiences were anecdotes that served as data from which to develop principles, whether about cities, economies, or other ecologies. For Jacobs, engaging in the world of work never meant passively accepting a job description. Indeed, Jacobs soon became involved in projects that she regarded as related to her work but that others, initially her employers and later the government, would find unwarranted, if not suspicious.

As she had hoped, hard work and initiative soon resulted in a promotion from secretary to editorial assistant, and with more responsibilities came a broader horizon of observation and experience. Among her first tasks was collecting information about the production rates of blast furnaces and other industry data by telephone, and her role soon expanded to the point she was making weekly trips to Philadelphia and traveling around the Northeast to gather news and information on market conditions from metals industry firms and scrap metal dealers. So although the subject matter was generally tedious and specialized, Jacobs began to develop an understanding of a regional economy—knowledge that she would draw on in *The Economy of Cities* and *Cities and the Wealth of Nations*—while also becoming familiar with the New York–Philadelphia–Washington, D.C., newsbeat that she would later cover as a writer for *Architectural Forum*.

Over the next two years, Jacobs was given additional responsibilities and independence, was promoted to associate editor, and developed the experience to take on advanced editorial roles with other magazines, including *Architectural Forum*, in the years ahead. While cutting her teeth on the long technical articles that were *Iron Age*'s lead stories, she was placed in charge of several small editorial departments. She visited the magazine's press in Philadelphia to handle last-minute layout and editing problems, and managed the magazine's Cleveland office when it was short-staffed during vacations. By late 1942, she had taken on such tasks as attending scientific conferences and important industrial meetings throughout New England, the Northeast, the Ohio Valley, and the Midwest, seeking out contributions from scientists and metallurgists directly, working with them on presenting their ideas, editing their manuscripts, and laying out their articles.

After the United States joined World War II following the bombing of Pearl Harbor on December 7, 1941, the metals industry became vitally important, and Jacobs found herself on the domestic front line. *Iron Age* was soon full of reports of wartime production; photographs of women building airplanes and fashioning bayonets; stories of the latest American, German, and Japanese airplanes, ships, and subs; and advertisements by the makers and suppliers of helmets, shell casings, and tanks. For the latest information, she visited contacts and officials of various government agencies in Washington, D.C., including the War Production Board, the Board of Economic Warfare, the War Department, the U.S. Navy, Department of the Interior, and Department of Labor. There she gathered news and discovered ideas for new articles and to assist her in interpreting facts gleaned elsewhere. As associate editor,

Jacobs had the autonomy to initiate and write her own features, technical articles, and special projects, and had the job security—or so she thought—to pursue activities of special interest to her.

Jacobs's initiative and interests were ultimately too much for an industrial trade magazine and for her editorial supervisor. He later told the Federal Bureau of Investigation (FBI) that Jacobs was "a very brilliant, intelligent young lady" who conducted herself well during her first few months of employment but whom he soon found to be "a trouble-maker and an agitator who would cause trouble no matter where she went." Although she could converse on any subject, he found her to be contrary and queer, sometimes found smoking a pipe in the office.[13] But it wasn't Jacobs's eccentric behavior that bothered him. When her boss eventually suggested that she find another job in November 1943, it was because Jacobs had become absorbed in projects extraneous to the magazine's primary business, was taking too much time away from her job to engage in these activities, and was no longer focused on her work.

Three projects preoccupied her during these years. Frustrated by the technical writing format of *Iron Age*, Jacobs became a regular freelance writer for the *New York Herald Tribune* starting in February 1942, eventually contributing more than 20 Sunday feature articles, which were frequently the cover stories of the science, education, or editorial sections. Further irritating her editors at *Iron Age*, these articles sometimes expanded on her research and work for the magazine, with the extracurricular goal of telling the larger human story beyond the industrial details that were *Iron Age*'s focus.

One of these, "Trylon's Steel Helps to Build Big New Nickel Plant in Cuba," told of the reuse of the steel from the New York World's Fair Trylon and other abandoned buildings to construct a new mining operation in Cuba. Jacobs had mentioned the new plant, whose production would offset a significant portion of the U.S. wartime nickel shortage, in her *Iron Age* article "Non-Ferrous Metals." There, however, she was not able to discuss the geographic, cultural, and economic transformation of the Cuban peninsula on which the plant and three new towns were being built. She was particularly interested in the way that the location of the plant had caused the towns to grow. "Until last May [1942]," she wrote, "the palm-covered peninsula was inhabited only by one family of Cuban subsistence farmers living in a tiny shack. Now 6,000 construction workers and engineers have built a railroad, pier, roads, and housing, and are working twenty hours a day pushing to completion about fifteen plant buildings."[14] The story had echoes of her essays on New York's working districts, recalled discussions of the TVA in her studies at Columbia, and anticipated her books on city economies.

Within the Chilton Company offices, a second project that preoccupied Jacobs was an effort to unionize the office's clerical workers. Although her editor later described these activities to the FBI as evidence of Jacobs's communist sympathies, he acknowledged that Jacobs had told him of her intentions at the time and that he had respected the workers' freedom of choice in the matter. This was not out of the ordinary: After the labor movements of the 1920s and 1930s, union membership was common in New York workplaces. Moreover, Jacobs's union, the Book and Magazine Local of the United Office and Professional Workers of America International, was hardly radical at a time when socialist and communist groups were a significant presence in the political landscape, even in city government.

Jacobs's primary interest in unionization, moreover, was fair pay for women. The war had transformed the domestic labor force and the economy; as Jacobs described in two of her freelance articles for the *New York Herald Tribune*, women were taking on the work of men who had gone overseas and were entering fields that were formerly the exclusive domain of men. In "Women Wanted to Fill 2,795 Kinds of Jobs," for example, Jacobs explained that according to the U.S. Employment Service, many jobs traditionally filled by men would be taken up by 5 million women entering the workforce in 1943. She observed that before the war "no women were listed as electricians, welders, draftsmen, or engine-lathe operators" in Employment Service directories. "Women are working now at all of these classifications," she continued, "and before the end of the war probably will have tackled the whole list and more." Jacobs had a laugh about the titles of some jobs listed in the service's directory—which included anti-squeak men, blow-off men, hotbed men, sweater men, keep-off men, and odd-shoe men—but jokes aside, she believed that "it can hardly be said that any occupation is absolutely unsuitable for women."[15] As Jacobs reported in "WAVES and WAACs Go Through Assignment Classification Mill," the trend was similar in the navy and army, where women's auxiliary units were "doing virtually every operation that male officers do ashore."[16]

Jacobs concluded that women worked as well as, or better than, men in industry, implying that a discussion of equal pay was sure to follow.

The third project related directly to her early interests in social and labor issues, and cities and urban economies: an effort to organize a campaign protesting the policies of the War Production Board and the state of Pennsylvania, which Jacobs believed were contributing to the economic decline of her hometown of Scranton. The effort also brought her interests in cities and activism together for the first time, resulting in an outcome that encouraged her later work, both writing and activism, on behalf of cities.

Jacobs's campaign began in late 1942, about a year into the war effort, and focused on bringing attention to Scranton as an attractive location for war production. She knew the city, of course, from growing up there, but she also understood the larger industrial landscape from her visits to metals industry firms in the Northeast and war production agencies in Washington, D.C. Further armed in April 1942 with a report by the Federal Anthracite Coal Commission, which recommended the Scranton region as a location for war plants, she helped to organize a targeted letter-writing campaign in conjunction with the Scranton Chamber of Commerce, a local foundation, and a local newspaper. As Jacobs reported in "30,000 Unemployed and 7,000 Empty Houses in Scranton, Neglected City"—a story that appeared, without a byline, in the "News of Industry" section of the *Iron Age* in March 1943— the city was one of "eighty-two paradoxical industrial areas of unemployment and empty houses" being underutilized at the same time as manpower and housing were in short supply in war production centers.[17]

Although it was decades before Jacobs wrote on urban and regional economies in *The Economy of Cities* and *Cities and Wealth*, having grown up in Scranton, she must have known already that despite the building of any new factories, the city's postwar fate would remain fundamentally unchanged. However, her first activist-writing project was a short-term success. She followed up on her *Iron Age* piece with a freelance story in the *New York Herald Tribune* and another in *Editor & Publisher*, a magazine for newspaper editors and executives, which prompted several hundred newspapers to pick up the story. The result was the building of a number of small factories and a large defense plant for the manufacture of wings for the Boeing B-29 in Scranton, and significant gratitude from the city. Soon after, a representative of the city's chamber of commerce recommended that March 25, 1943, the date of Jacobs's first article, should "go down in the history of Scranton as IRON AGE Day, for that day marks the turning point in Scranton's history."[18] Had her article been bylined, it might have been "Jane Butzner Day."

## JANE JACOBS: BLACKLISTED PROPAGANDIST

Whether Jacobs's colleagues at *Iron Age* knew or cared about her efforts in Scranton, in the autumn of 1943, she left the magazine and joined the war effort as a propaganda writer for the Office of War Information (OWI). In November 1943, she signed the OWI's declaration of secrecy, which charged her to bear true faith and allegiance to the United States of America, to serve the country honestly and faithfully against its enemies, and to keep secret any information about the OWI's purposes and methods of propaganda and psychological warfare. She started work as a feature writer for the OWI's Overseas Division and worked as a writer and editor for the U.S. government for nine years, first for the OWI and then for the State Department, which took over the OWI's operations when the world war became a cold war.

Jacobs's work for the OWI and the State Department was, by nature, shrouded in secrecy. Her work as a propagandist and the circumstances surrounding her departure were not easy subjects for casual conversation in the early 1960s, when there was first interest in her early career. However, her propaganda work, at least what is known of it, was not especially cunning. During World War II, she may have contributed to reports that overstated U.S. war production, military readiness, and the like. But much of her work was more public relations than misinformation and consisted of telling the story of the United States, its government, people, and way of life—a story that she believed in. She sometimes worked with overseas intelligence services to monitor and respond to false information in foreign media, whether borne of ignorance or counterintelligence. She was sometimes engaged, in other words, in what she later described as the "Guardian moral syndrome," which applied particularly in wartime. Characteristics of the guardian mentality, as she defined it in *Systems of Survival*, included exhibiting prowess, being obedient and disciplined, respecting hierarchy, promoting monumentality, maintaining territory, and deceiving for the sake of the task—qualities necessarily exemplified in her work for the OWI.[19] Although writing that book from the point of view of a "Trader" and the "Commercial moral syndrome," she understood quite a lot about its counterpart, the Guardian moral syndrome, from personal experience.

Equally significant from the point of view of her biography were Jacobs's professional experiences during her time with the OWI and the State Department. Less than a year into her work for the OWI, she was handling many of the bureau's top assignments, including special psychological warfare articles for European outposts, and her bureau chief observed that she had developed into "one of the mainstays of the feature-writing staff." Two things, he noted, had been responsible for this: Jacobs's "quick grasp of the propaganda job to be done, and her ability to do a fast, efficient and well-handled piece of work with any assignment given her."[20]

During a nine-month hiatus as the OWI's operations were transferred to the State Department in 1946, Jacobs did freelance work. In October 1946, she returned and continued her rapid rise through the editorial hierarchy, although under the very different circumstances of the Cold War. She was rehired as a staff writer—more or less the same job she'd had before—for a new publication called *Amerika Illiustrirovannoye* (*America Illustrated*), a State Department magazine to be distributed in the USSR. The magazine was the outcome of an exchange-of-information agreement between Roosevelt and Stalin at the Yalta Conference in early 1945. Full of pictures of typical American scenes—Arizona deserts, TVA dams, the white steeples of a Connecticut town, Radio City, bluegrass country, the Senate in session, Manhattan's garment district (likely one of Jacobs's contributions)—*Amerika's* mission was to present a sympathetic and appealing vision of how Americans lived, worked, and played.[21] According to a contemporary reviewer, the approach was "strictly factual, never boasting, and never political. Never are there any direct criticisms of the worker's paradise."[22] Comparing *Soviet Life* and *Amerika* in 1956, the *Christian Science Monitor* observed, "Both put their countries' best foot forward. Both emphasize the good things of life, the cultural interests of their people, their sports, and home life. Both steer clear of any political arguments or dialectics."[23]

Unlike *Soviet Life* in the United States, however, *Amerika* quickly became a popular and coveted object in the USSR. The magazine was lavishly produced, and in addition to specially written or commissioned articles, *Amerika* reproduced articles from a variety of U.S. publications such as *Life*, *Fortune*, and *Architectural Forum*. This broadened Jacobs's familiarity with the New York publishing world and provided her with the connections to find new work when the time came.

Of equal significance, *Amerika* provided Jacobs with the opportunity to write about a wide variety of subjects of interest to her, including architecture and one of the first comprehensive surveys of housing and urban redevelopment projects that took place around the time of the passage of the U.S. Housing Act of 1949—subjects that she would later focus on at *Architectural Forum*.

By the late 1940s, Jacobs had been promoted to editor and soon thereafter to a State Department editor-in-chief position, in which she planned future articles; reviewed story ideas; worked closely with the copy and publications editors and the art director; made critical analysis of all copy by staff, senior writers, and outside contractors; and interviewed, hired, and supervised freelance writers. She wrote in explanation of a request for promotion in September 1949, "My supervisory and planning responsibilities have consistently grown and now occupy approximately seventy-five percent of my time; the remainder being devoted to developing and writing of complex articles."[24] Before starting at *Architectural Forum*, Jacobs had come a long way from her first freelance work of the mid-1930s, and these aspects of her professional background help to explain why she was able to move so easily into a senior editorial position at *Architectural Forum*—a circumstance that biographies of Jacobs have failed to adequately consider.

But having reached a milestone of professional responsibility—and having done so by serving her country with the sincere and committed purpose of telling the story of America—it must have been a distressing surprise for Jacobs to come under the scrutiny of the FBI and the Loyalty Security Board in the late 1940s for suspected "un-American" sympathies. She had, after all, not just earned the praise of her superiors, she had written a book on the U.S. Constitution! Nevertheless, whether or not she knew it for certain, she was among those employees of the State Department who had originally transferred over from the war agencies who were the specific focus of Senator Joseph McCarthy's demands for further investigation. He sincerely believed that State Department employees other than the alleged spy Alger Hiss harbored communist sympathies.

Jacobs was, in fact, investigated for years, and by no less a detective than FBI director J. Edgar Hoover himself, who personally managed her investigations. Although the FBI's initial investigation of her was pro forma, a requirement of the U.S. Information and Educational Exchange Act of 1948, Jacobs had made an innocent but irreparable error: She had listed Alger Hiss, a State Department acquaintance, as a reference on one of her many government-required forms for promotion. The FBI's further investigations also revealed that in the months between her employment at the OWI and the State Department, Jacobs and her husband had applied a number of times for visas to the USSR, which was then still an ally. Once again, the reasons were innocent. Jacobs had specialized in Russian affairs during her time with the OWI, which was why she was hired for *Amerika Illiustrirovannoye*, and while she was freelancing between jobs, she had pitched a story on Siberia to *Natural History* magazine, where she wanted to find a permanent position after the OWI was shut down. Jacobs had little opportunity to explain this, however. The FBI's many field investigations—which involved interviews with present and former neighbors, landlords, coworkers, employers, and acquaintances—produced a picture of an eccentric resident of bohemian Greenwich Village, the home of many known and suspected radicals, who was known to have been involved in union activities, sometimes in violation of federal policies; to have registered for the American Labor Party; and to have been intimately involved in writing for a Soviet audience.

Ultimately, the FBI's investigation of Jacobs became moot, as the Red Scare forced the closure of the State Department's entire publications operation in New York and the temporary suspension of *Amerika*. Rather than follow her insecure job to Washington, D.C., Jacobs resigned from government employment in April 1952. While it is not clear if Jacobs was aware of the extent of Hoover's investigation, it seems clear that the combination of the secret nature of her government work in the 1940s, the taint of McCarthyism in the 1950s, and the anti-establishmentarianism of the 1960s all conspired to make much of Jacobs's early career better left unspoken. In light of her genuine commitment to American democracy and her abhorrence of the Soviet system, the experience left her with pent-up anger toward government bureaucracy—which she would later release against the urban renewal regime.

## JANE JACOBS: CITY PLANNING IDEALIST

*Architectural Forum* editor Douglas Haskell hired Jacobs in May 1952, just as he was about to announce a new editorial policy that would emphasize architectural criticism and include a new focus on urban redevelopment. Although previously unacknowledged in Jacobs's biographies, Haskell's editorial policy and his personal support would directly shape her career, writing style, and eventually the writing of *Death and Life*. Like Jacobs, Haskell did not have training in either architecture or city planning, but since beginning his career as a freelance architectural critic in the 1920s, he had sought to push the boundaries of American architectural criticism, which had been constrained by the threat of libel suits and gentleman's agreements among architects. By the early 1950s, when he could define his own editorial policy, he looked for staff who could advance this cause. In Jacobs, he quickly found not only a keen architectural critic but also someone who would find a new direction for criticism in writing about urban redevelopment, and take his editorial agenda in unexpected and sometimes unwelcome directions.

In the early 1950s—when there was little evidence of the failures of urban redevelopment in the form of built projects—Jacobs, Haskell, and others who believed in cities backed the federal urban renewal policies that were recognized as failures only in retrospect. Both Jacobs and Haskell were urban minded at a time when "decentralization" was a national trend. Both had come to New York because they loved the city, and this predilection manifested itself in Haskell's agenda for *Architectural Forum* and Jacobs's writing: The magazine did not seek to advance the cause of garden cities, new towns, and suburbs; and Jacobs wouldn't have worked there if it did.

At the time, the alternative to decentralization was to support policies that directed investment into cities, not exurban projects. Although one was the product of a Democratic administration and the other of a Republican administration, the U.S. Housing Acts of 1949 and 1954 were bipartisan in the sense that they contained provisions that satisfied both those who wanted to see cities rehabilitated and those interested in suburban real estate development. But when the choice was between supporting cities and supporting decentralization, it should come as little surprise that Jacobs was a passionate advocate for cities, even if the promising policies for the renewal of American cities were untested.

Jacobs's early writing for *Architectural Forum* reflected her personal idealization of urban renewal and the related field of city planning, and the shared national optimism. In one of her earliest articles for *Architectural Forum*, for example, when Jacobs was still focused on the hospital architecture topics that she had been hired to cover, she couldn't help but express her hope for the future of cities. Although her subject was the accomplished hospital architect Isadore Rosenfield, it was Rosenfield's "city planner approach" that she found most admirable in her September 1952 article "Rosenfield and His Hospitals: He Approaches His Jobs Like a City Planner." Whereas the typical architect works with the program he is given, she observed, the "city planner gets a problem and he has to start from scratch," coming to terms with the problem, doing the research, and only then determining a unique solution. "Working either as a consultant or architect," Jacobs wrote admiringly, "Rosenfield uses the city planner approach, does his own studies right down to digging out the facts on family income in the community. His facility with this kind of research comes out of his three years' training as a social scientist. He is suspicious of all rules of thumb and initial assumptions."[25] Influenced by her early interest in the life sciences, Jacobs clearly associated Rosenfield's inductive methodology —which was very similar to what she later advocated in the last chapter of *Death and Life*—with the larger field of city planning.

Over the next few years, while Jacobs took on the role of *Architectural Forum*'s specialist on the regional shopping center, a new postwar building type, she continued to think about the city and to idealize city planning considerations, in this case in relation to shopping center design. In her March 1953 feature article, "New Thinking on Shopping Centers," she wrote that the best shopping center planners had become "community planners in self-defense" and described rather uncritically how some developers hosted community-planning meetings in order to generate public support. "Here is the idealism of town planning actually become reality, not another buried report," she wrote sincerely, "because it fits the cold facts of good merchandising."[26]

In June 1954, she similarly described Victor Gruen's Northland shopping center in Detroit as "a new thing in modern town planning" and praised the ways the design, with its traditionally "urban 'market town' plan," learned from and imitated traditional urbanism. Moreover, at the time, Jacobs sincerely believed that downtown, which was being threatened by exurban development, had something to learn from suburbs and shopping malls. She observed that "every unplanned suburban strip losing out to a planned shopping center is a lesson in survival that cannot be ignored" and concluded that "the first—the most elementary—lesson for downtown is simply the importance of planning."[27] The notions that great cities could learn something from the suburbs and that "monopolistic" shopping center patterns, as she later described them, were ideas that Jacobs later disowned and explicitly argued against in *Death and Life*. However, in the mid-1950s, she still regarded city planning as fundamental and necessary.

Although her views later changed, it was through such interests and writing experiences that Jacobs became *Architectural Forum*'s urban redevelopment specialist. Writing about architecture and suburban development as she did—with an eye to the city—her assignments segued naturally into writing about urban redevelopment. In the mid-1950s, she visited and wrote about redevelopment in Philadelphia, Cleveland, Washington, D.C., Fort Worth, Texas, and New York. Her understanding of cities and redevelopment evolved all the while, with her opinions about the city planners and urban redevelopments that she wrote about being mostly positive. In Cleveland, she admired the work and ambitions of city planners Ernest Bohn and James Lister and Allan Jacobs's design for the Green Valley development. In Washington, D.C., she observed that the city had many of the same problems as other American cities—a "choked downtown, haphazard suburban sprawl, blight at the heart"—but she praised the plans and designs of I. M. Pei, Harry Weese, Frederick Gutheim, and Willo von Molke for creating a new "architecture of city space" that respected "old city patterns" without mimicking traditional architecture.[28] Similarly, in Fort Worth, Texas, Jacobs greatly admired the combination of imagination and realism that Ed Contini and Victor Gruen brought to bear on the problem of automobiles in the city. She also admired their renewal plan for the city, which was based on intimate and detailed knowledge of the redevelopment area, and respected and provided for "the variety of healthy city growth." As with Rosenfield, she praised not only their research but "the way the planner's part [was] conceived." Unlike the authoritarian and paternalistic planners whom Jacobs would later attack, Gruen's team "resisted the temptation of confusing their wishes with the will of the citizenry." Moreover, "there was no attempt to force it over or finagle it backstage"—as Jacobs had seen done in Washington, D.C., and as she would later observe as Robert Moses's modus operandi in New York.[29] Indeed, even after Jacobs had become disillusioned with city planning and redevelopment, in *Death and Life* she remained a strong advocate of Gruen's and Contini's ideas.

Despite the evidence in *Death and Life*, among the greatest theoretical influences on Jacobs's thinking in the early 1950s were city planner Ed Bacon's and architect Louis Kahn's ideas about the city, and their plans for Philadelphia. As *Architectural Forum*'s primary contact for Philadelphia architects, she spent a great deal of time there and got to know both the city and the architects well. She was charmed by Kahn, quickly recognized his architectural genius, and recommended that *Architectural Forum* publish articles on his early projects. She was also aware of the influence of Kahn's urban design studies for Philadelphia on Gruen's ideas for Fort Worth, Texas, and she may indeed have been the link between the two. But she was most inspired by Bacon's and Kahn's ideas of the "living city" and their related approach to redevelopment, which respected neighborhood social structure and building fabric, and emphasized landscape and urban design strategies over architectural interventions. Although Jacobs later took some pleasure in repeating the anti–urban renewal rallying cry "Fry Bacon!" in *Death and Life*, she knew that Ed Bacon was a very different city planner than Robert Moses and that "The Philadelphia Cure" for urban decay was very different from the "blockbusting approach" in New York, as these local methods were described by *Architectural Forum*'s writers and editors. She quoted Bacon in 1955 as stating an idea that she believed in: that the "efficiency and order which the planner desires is less important than the preservation of individual democratic liberties and, where the two are in conflict, the demands of the democratic process must prevail."[30]

Even more significant, Ed Bacon's idea that cities and their neigh-borhoods are "dynamic organisms which have within themselves the seeds of self-regeneration" is one that Jacobs claimed as her own.[31] This idea was a logical extension of her interests in geography and ecology, but Bacon cannot be easily ruled out as a catalyst critical to the devel-opment of concepts central to *Death and Life*. In 1955, Bacon showed her that many city neighborhoods have "the latent capacity to restore themselves"—a vital urban process that Jacobs later described in *Death and Life* as "unslumming."[32] This idea was at the heart of Jacobs's un-derstanding of the city as a complex and dynamic organism. It was not only the basis of her "death and life" thesis; Bacon's regenerating-seed metaphor also found new life in the concluding sentence of Jacobs's great book, where she wrote that "lively, diverse, intense cities contain the seeds of their own regeneration, with energy enough to carry over for problems and needs outside themselves."[33]

Jacobs's opinions of urban renewal and city planners soon changed, of course, and it was at that point that Jacobs's writing and her biography became better known. While her support of urban redevelopment had been unremarkable, her criticism of it was much more noteworthy. Lewis Mumford later recalled Jacobs's debut at the first Harvard Urban Design Conference in 1956 in his otherwise scathing critique of *Death and Life*: "A few years ago, Mrs. Jacobs stepped into prominence at a planners' con-ference at Harvard. Into the foggy atmosphere of professional jargon that usually envelops such meetings, she blew like a fresh offshore breeze."[34]

As Mumford's comment suggests, Jacobs's contributions to planning the-ory and urban design were significant as much for their timing as for their content, and also because she was one of very few women in the field. Indeed, even though Jacobs was a woman without any formal training in architecture or planning, her comments about the destruction of relationships between city fabric and public space by urban renewal projects still made a significant impression at the Harvard planners' conference—and this was because she already knew as much or more about the impacts of these projects as any-one in the room. Having written about urban redevelopment since soon after the passage of the U.S. Housing Act of 1949 for *Amerika* and followed the progress of projects from the planning stage to construction for *Architectural*

*Forum*, she had a largely unrivaled store of knowledge. Moreover, she was personally familiar with the heavy-handedness of renewal projects through the Greenwich Village campaign to stop Robert Moses's redevelopment of Washington Square—an experience with one of the earliest episodes in the protest movement, which few could then claim.

It was with that early and protracted neighborhood fight, which Jacobs referred to in *Death and Life* and elsewhere, that her idealism began to fade. She wrote the following to New York mayor Robert F. Wagner and Manhattan borough president Hulan Jack in a 1955 letter-writing campaign organized by neighborhood activist Shirley Hayes:

> My husband and I are among the citizens who truly believe in New York—to the extent that we have bought a home in the heart of the city and remodeled it with a lot of hard work (transforming it from slum property) and are raising our three children here. It is very discouraging to try to do our best to make the city more habitable, and then to learn that the city itself is thinking up schemes to make it uninhabitable.[35]

But more significant, in early 1956, when there was little evidence of completed renewal projects elsewhere, Jacobs was familiar with the plight of a neighborhood that was of interest to few outsiders or reporters, New York's East Harlem, the nation's urban renewal guinea pig. By January 1956, when Jacobs first visited East Harlem, 10 housing projects had consumed 57 blocks, more than two-thirds of East Harlem.[36] Not long after, the number of projects had climbed, and social worker Ellen Lurie, one of Jacobs's most important contacts and influences, observed, "In this proportionately small section [of the city], fourteen public-housing projects have already been or soon will be constructed. But no self-respecting laboratory technician would dare subject one guinea pig to fourteen identical tests in order to discover the efficacy of a method."[37] Lurie had detailed documentation of every neighborhood store and social club that was destroyed, along with the old storefront buildings that were razed for the new monolithic housing projects, and it was these studies that formed the basis of Jacobs's Harvard conference paper and marked the end of her belief in the "city planner approach."

## JANE JACOBS: CITY PLANNING AND URBAN DESIGN THEORIST

In the late 1950s, when Jacobs began the project that became *Death and Life*, she was not just angry with city planners and urban renewal agencies, she was also rather angry with herself. As she later told her friend Grady Clay, who was at work on related projects, she felt personally responsible and guilty for having believed in urban renewal. "I had a pervading uneasiness about the way the rebuilding of the city was going, augmented by some feeling of personal guilt, I suppose, or at least personal involvement," she wrote him in 1959, while at work on the book. "The reason for this was that in all sincerity I had been writing for *Forum* about how great various redevelopment plans were going to be," she continued. "Then I began to see some of these things built. They weren't delightful, they weren't fine, and they were obviously never going to work right . . . I began to get this very uneasy feeling that what sounded logical in planning theory and what looked splendid on paper was not logical in real life at all, or at least in city real life, and not splendid at all when in use."[38]

In other words, Jacobs's motivations were deeper and more personal than previous biographies have acknowledged, and so were her experiences and her ambitions for a better understanding of cities and their design and planning. Moreover, her opportunity to make a contribution did not come about because she was an amateur, as the prevailing stereotype holds, but because, by early 1958, she was already recognized as one of the most knowledgeable writers in the country on redevelopment and the city. Although her ideas about cities were fundamentally transformed in the late 1950s, her writings and thinking about the city spanned 20 years, and it was this body of experience that led to her opportunity to be part of a historic grant initiative funded by the Rockefeller Foundation, which helped establish the new field of urban design and produced such seminal works as Kevin Lynch's *Image of the City* (1960).

Although Jacobs's battles with Robert Moses and her other activist projects of the 1960s and 1970s were legendary, these were motivated by a memory of having once believed in urban renewal herself, and by a great conviction about the need to pursue an alternative to the "blockbusting" approach. This conviction was founded on long experience, the knowledge of alternative approaches pursued by more mindful city planners and urban designers in other cities, and by her belief in the theoretical foundation for a new urbanism that she had developed in *Death and Life*. As she wrote to Chadbourne Gilpatric, her contact at the Rockefeller Foundation in 1959 while she was at work on *Death and Life*, "This book is neither a retelling in new form of things already said, nor an expansion and enlargement of previously worked out basic ground, but it is an attempt to make what amounts to a different system of thought about the great city."[39]

Jacobs's system of thought about the great city—an understanding of the city's diversity, complexity, and self-organizing properties, and the fragile ecological relationships between city fabric, public and private space, and social life—have become our own. But this system of thought did not emerge spontaneously. It was based on Jacobs's belief in what city planning and design should ideally be and, in a few inspiring cases, already was.

# An Australian Jane Jacobs

JANE M. JACOBS

## DISAMBIGUATION

Most of us in the field of urban studies and planning operate in the aura of Jane Jacobs and her landmark book *The Death and Life of Great American Cities* (1961).[1] Some more so than others. Myself more than most. I was not named after *The* Jane Jacobs, as I have come to refer to her. My nonacademic, suburb-dwelling Australian parents knew nothing of Jane Jacobs and her work, and I was born a few years shy of the year *Death and Life* was published and Jacobs began to accrue her global notoriety. The shared name is a coincidence that would not have mattered if I had not had a career as an academic human geographer who, among other things, works on the city.

Sharing Jane Jacobs's name has produced confusion and many instances of professional misrecognition. Managing such confusion is an everyday part of my working life, and the need has abated only in a minor way since Jane Jacobs's death. I routinely find myself disappointing excited students who think they have the good fortune to be in the class of *The* Jane Jacobs. At conferences when unknowing colleagues approach me, like fans, and offer praise and thanks for *Death and Life*, I offer a carefully cultivated set of responses that ensure neither they nor I feel too foolish. In these encounters I am implicated in a ludicrous bathos: Because I am not *The* Jane Jacobs, I inevitably force a transition from the exalted to the commonplace. I routinely help the transition along by offering these disappointed colleagues various comic prefixes and suffixes by which they might place me in relation to *The* Jane Jacobs: "Oh no, I am the *other* Jane Jacobs," or "Oh no, I am Jane Jacobs the Younger," or if I am particularly tired of it all, "Don't you know? I am Jane Jacobs the Lesser." As my own, far more moderate, reputation grew among colleagues, I found they, too, had to take on the confusion by adding qualifications when they referenced my work: "the Australian Jane Jacobs," "the postcolonial Jane Jacobs."

The context in which I was introduced to *Death and Life* was a southern city in 1970s Australia—a place that was geographically far from New York, although linguistically proximate, being part of the Anglophone world. I was an undergraduate student in geography at the University of Adelaide. My urban geography professor was Blair Badcock, whose tutelage was dedicated to getting his variously receptive students to grasp the relationship between urban processes and uneven outcomes. Like many such courses, the course we read with him was the basis for a book, which appeared in 1984 with the title *Unfairly Structured Cities*.[2] It was through that course that I first heard of *Death and Life*. I bought my one and only copy a little later, when I was undertaking my first postgraduate degree at the same university and starting to glimpse the possibility of an academic career. The copy I bought was a battered secondhand one. I did not read it immediately, and I have never read it cover to cover. Yet it was one of a few books I took to London when I did a Ph.D. on urban heritage. In that research, my reading of *Death and Life* was still slight and strategic, and I tended to use it as background to more recent and substantively argued cases about why heritage matters. As an academic teaching an urban course I have more routinely and systematically turned to *Death and Life*. Reflecting on my own use of *Death and Life*, it is apt that my copy came to me secondhand, for I have always drawn on the ideas contained within it in a retrospective mode. And it is certain that to understand contemporary sensibilities in urban planning, we need to know something of the turning point that *Death and Life* articulated.

Where does my now yellowed and battered copy of this influential book sit among the many thousands that have been produced and circulated around the globe? More specifically, how was this book and its ideas received in the Australia of the 1960s, 1970s, and after? I have not been able to find data on sales figures for *Death and Life* in Australia, although the Australian urban historian Hugh Stretton notes that "it climbed *Time*'s best-seller list, and an English hardback and a Pelican paperback were in the Melbourne bookshops for a decade."[3] To chart the reception of *Death and Life* in Australia, it is useful to establish who was available to receive such a book. In what follows I want to talk about three distinct types of audiences: professional planners, scholarly academics, and activists.

## PLANNING RECEPTION

Let us turn first to planning, the very profession that Jacobs's book critiqued and sought to reform. It seems that *Death and Life*, in the first decades after it was published, was largely ignored by the Australian bureaucratic urban planning profession. In his influential book *Ideas for Australian Cities*, urban historian and commentator Hugh Stretton notes explicitly the ignorance of the book and its ideas among professional urban planners: "The relevant state authorities didn't keep qualified librarians, and none of them appeared to have heard of the book or given attention to its own or any other version of its serious and complex argument."[4] He concludes that urban planning practice in 1960s and 1970s Australia remained wedded to far simpler theories of comprehensive infrastructural planning. Historical geographer Margo Huxley, who in the early 1970s was working with the planning department of the South Melbourne Council, recalls that there was little evidence of the thinking of Jane Jacobs in the everyday work of bureaucratic planning.[5] Similarly, the Australian-trained planning scholar Leonie Sandercock has reflected that Jacobs was not part of the canon of planning education in Australia, which for many years was framed by the country's history as a British settler colony and its continuing membership in the Commonwealth: "She was not 'one of them' and Oz planning education was dominated by the texts of male British expats working in Oz."[6] Be that as it may, the experience of American cities offered Australian planners both negative warnings and positive solutions.[7] *Death and Life* was undoubtedly influential in this respect, although that influence has been largely overlooked in systematic accounts of Australian planning's assimilation of American ideas. As one planner noted, the influence of the writings of Jane Jacobs on Australian planning has been largely "left unremarked."[8]

Sandercock's published reflection on planning education in Australia cites *Death and Life* explicitly when discussing the emergence of a local Australian mood of suspicion around technical city builders (planners, architects, and engineers). "The 1970s," she notes, "was a decade of questioning from without and agonising from within the 'profession.'" It saw the proliferation of what she dubs "paraplanning" courses in universities and colleges of advanced education, which sought to "address the deficiencies in previous planning education."[9] This reform was very much a reevaluation of top-down, comprehensive planning, and a move toward putting the neighborhood, community, and local context center stage in planning processes. "Civic design" or neighborhood planning courses, for example, were gaining popularity and offered Jacobs's *Death and Life* a receptive audience, although more as a "philosophical" influence than as a practical guide.[10] One Australian planning commentator noted in 1973, "Jane Jacobs changed the thinking of a good many planners when she took them to task for sterile planning and a total inability to see or to understand the urban environment as people living in it did."[11]

## Academic Reception

Academics writing on the Australian city in the decades immediately after *Death and Life* was published were receptive to its ideas, although to argue that Jacobs was a major force would be an overstatement. Critical academic thinking about cities in the 1970s and 1980s in Australia, as elsewhere, was shaped by the critical insights of Marxist political economy.[12] As Kilmartin, Thorns, and Burke note in *Social Theory and the Australian City*, a political-economy perspective sets aside and assumes conservative any approach that "attributes to space, buildings and population concentrations a life and logic of their own."[13] Jacobs's account of the city, with its emphasis on the creative power of conviviality and sociality and the disadvantages of comprehensive built planning, could readily be seen as a footnote to this more substantive critique of the city in the course of capitalist development. Margo Huxley commented that Jacobs's ideas tended to be characterized as "woolly liberalism," "journalistic," or "ideological," rather than "properly theoretical."[14]

That said, *Death and Life* is routinely given a passing nod in many of the key urban texts of the time. One issue facing Australian cities to which the arguments of *Death and Life* were immediately attached was that of suburbanization. Speculative land acquisition and development on the urban fringes were rife during the 1960s and early 1970s, leading to rapid suburbanization. The social impacts of that development were felt unevenly. In the context of what is known popularly as a home-owning nation, the sprawling suburbs of Australia—although a material manifestation of middle-class ideologies of urban living—came to be populated by a debt-encumbered but aspirational lower-middle and working class. It is in describing such social impacts that, for example, Blair Badcock's *Unfairly Structured Cities* draws on the ideas of Jane Jacobs. Referring specifically to the isolation of the suburbs for women, Badcock notes the poor "physical form of postwar suburbs in Australia and the United States," blaming it on "the abdication of their designers (all male) to the automobile." He goes on: "Jane Jacobs (1961) had a different focus in eulogizing the richness of social relations within Greenwich Village in the heart of Manhattan, but many of the qualities she praised are missing from the postwar suburb."[15]

In his influential book *Ideas for Australian Cities*—first self-published in 1970 but given mainstream publishing in various editions throughout the 1970s and 1980s—historian Hugh Stretton judges "the more original and important" part of Jacobs's argument about urban planning to be her understanding of the "complex social economy of the old-style built-up street." But he concludes that in the Australian context "the argument has limited application. It is no help to the planning of low-density suburbs, or to any planning for segregated people who refuse to mix. It is short of strategic alternatives. . . . Some of its concerns are peculiarly American; some of its precautions Australians don't need."[16]

Stretton was not alone in his stance toward Jacobs's ideas. Another influential urban scholar, Pat Troy, for many years head of the Urban Research Unit at the Australian National University, bought his copy of *Death and Life* soon after the first edition was published but found its ideas to be a "distraction" because they were so American and not relevant to "the way our cities had grown or where they were going."[17]

Although such influential Australian urban scholars were and remain circumspect about the relevance of *Death and Life*, it is clear the book had a certain status that could not be refused. For example, when Hugh Stretton's student Leonie Sandercock set off from Adelaide for Canberra in 1971 to undertake a Ph.D. with the Australian National University's Urban Research Unit, Stretton handed her a copy of Lewis Mumford's *The City in History* and recommended she read Jacobs's *Death and Life*.[18] And today Sandercock attributes her own lively and engaging style of writing on planning to the template offered by Jacobs in *Death and Life*.[19]

## ACTIVIST RECEPTION

In the 1970s in Australia, *Death and Life* found a more emphatic and enthusiastic audience among an activist public that was beginning to complain vociferously about comprehensive planning interventions. As Stretton puts it: "This international best seller is the most readable of all statements of the case against the bulldozer."[20] It was in the older, inner-city areas of Australian cities, where potent battles were emerging, that the ideas of Jane Jacobs made sense. These battles were between, on the one side, planners and developers pushing through slum clearance, high-rise housing development, and freeway construction, and on the other, a motley coalition of interests ranging from residents to intellectuals to trade unionists. These activists were receptive to Jacobs's arguments. Hugh Stretton notes one such devoted inner-city readership in 1970s Melbourne: "The book was for some years the bible of the Carlton and Richmond intellectuals who read claret-stained copies of it, sometimes by the light of candles stuck in bottles, in their refurbished terrace houses under the long shadow of the Housing Commission [high-rise housing] towers."[21]

And similarly, Leonie Sandercock reflected: "1971–74, it was a pivotal moment in terms of a rising civil society opposition to planning by the state, particularly the plans in each capital city for massive freeway networks and high-rise urban redevelopment for public housing. These were exactly the things Jacobs was fighting in NY, the demolition of neighbourhoods, and it gave us a vocabulary for the fight that ensued through the '70s and beyond."[22]

As far as I can determine, Jane Jacobs never visited Australia or saw an Australian city. That said, the ideas contained within *Death and Life* circulated in Australia, albeit unevenly. For professional urban planners, *Death and Life* was a bothersome polemic, but one that chimed with local complaints that ultimately forced planning reform away from comprehensive planning. For political economy–focused urban scholars of the city, it was a mere footnote to their more evidently theoretical efforts. For activists, it provided a vocabulary for articulating what was wrong in some parts of some Australian cities. It is easy to assume a book as influential as *Death and Life* is a global phenomenon, and in some respects it is. But even the most influential of books is also always a situated-knowledge production: *Death and Life* was produced somewhere, and as it traveled elsewhere it encountered different urban histories and alternative urban aspirations and was made different. *Death and Life* did not offer a discrete policy package that traveled by way of some transparent and readily mapped model of diffusion. Rather, as I have sought to show, it was a book that had diffuse effects. Yet today there is little doubt that you, like me, operate in the irrefutable aura of Jane Jacobs's *Death and Life of Great American Cities*.[23]

# THE LITERARY CRAFT OF JANE JACOBS

## JAMIN CREED ROWAN

In July 1959, Jane Jacobs wrote Chadbourne Gilpatric—associate director of the Humanities Division at the Rockefeller Foundation—to request additional funding to help her complete *The Death and Life of Great American Cities*. A year earlier, the Rockefeller Foundation had, at the urging of Gilpatric, given Jacobs a $10,000 grant, but progress on her manuscript had been unexpectedly slow. Projecting a May 1960 completion, Jacobs provided Gilpatric with an "accounting of the sum" that she would need to get her "through this period." In addition to asking for money to cover her salary losses while she wrote full-time, Jacobs requested funds to rent an office. At some point during the previous year, she had "found it necessary to hire a room to work in," where she would be "uninterrupted by people, telephone, etc." She had been renting space "in a rooming house costing $45 a month," but, she informed Gilpatric, "that building has been sold and I have to find another, which I expect will be about the same rent."[1] When the Rockefeller Foundation gave Jacobs most of what she asked for, she rented an office in Greenwich Village on the second floor of a two-story building situated at the intersection of West Fourth Street, Seventh Avenue, and Christopher Street. A quick four-block walk from her home at 555 Hudson Street, Jacobs's new office was located above a gym and directly across the corridor from the Music Society's headquarters.[2]

The image of Jacobs hammering away at a typewriter in her second-floor studio at 225 West Fourth Street offers a valuable addition to the personas through which the public has typically understood her. While many tend to conceive of Jacobs primarily as a community activist and urban planner who happened to write very well, she thought of herself first and foremost as a writer. When Leticia Kent referred to her as an "urbanologist" during an interview for *Vogue*, Jacobs bristled and said, "Please don't describe me as an urbanologist." Asked for a more suitable label, Jacobs responded matter-of-factly, "An author."[3] Jacobs identified herself as a writer to the extent that she would get a bit cranky when the demands of community activism kept her away from her desk. She frequently turned down speaking invitations and other flattering engagements for fear that they would cut too deeply into her writing time. "You either do your work or you're a celebrity," Jacobs once quipped, adding, "I'd rather do my work."[4]

Given Jacobs's repeated attempts to define herself as an author, it is surprising that critics have not paid more explicit attention to the literariness of her work. Readers have frequently described her words as prophetic, but the model of author as prophet is an inadequate one. It implies that Jacobs's message transcends its medium and that, rather than make conscious literary choices, she thoughtlessly transcribed bursts of inspiration. When reviewers and critics have, on occasion, taken Jacobs seriously as a writer, they have done so by casting her as the literary progeny of 19th-century writers such as Henry David Thoreau, Harriet Beecher Stowe, and Walt Whitman, or by positioning her at the center of a 1960s protest-literature cohort that includes Rachel Carson, Betty Friedan, Michael Harrington, and Ralph Nader.[5] While grouping Jacobs with these writers nudges her into an American literary tradition in which she belongs, these comparisons are driven by attentiveness more to her countercultural message than to her prose style.

Although she had no doubt read Thoreau and Stowe, and was certainly aware of the work of her contemporaries, Jacobs's literary form and style draw much more directly upon the popular vernaculars swirling around the mid-century city. I contend that Jacobs picked up her literary craft not from the other urban planners with whom she is so often compared but from city journalists, hard-boiled novelists, settlement-house writers, and others who wrote for the general public. *Death and Life* appealed to as many readers as it did in large part because it resonated with the linguistic and narrative structures through which those readers had come to know urban life. Jacobs may not have been, as Christopher Klemek, Peter Laurence, and others have recently demonstrated, unique in her critique of urban renewal.[6] There were, as she openly admitted to Gilpatric, "quite a number of people today looking at the city in the same way I am doing."[7] In fact, many of her ideas closely resembled the responses of New York City's municipal leaders in the late 1950s to the increasingly visible social consequences of urban renewal.[8] Jacobs was, however, unrivaled among urban planners, architects, and elected officials in her ability to articulate these shared ideas about urban life in a way that persuaded a great number of people to invest in them. Jacobs's genius perhaps lies less in her system of thought than in her ability to package those thoughts into an accessible literary and narrative form.

## DEATH AND LIFE'S LITERARY FORM

When pitching the idea of a "book about certain characteristics of the big city" to Gilpatric and the Rockefeller Foundation, Jacobs explained that she would be writing for the "general interested citizen, rather than writing for the specialist."[9] Given her extensive training in city journalism, Jacobs was well prepared to make good on her promise to produce a book that would appeal to a wide range of readers. While both writing and editing for urban literary institutions such as *Vogue*, *Fortune*, *Architectural Forum*, the *New York Herald Tribune*, and the *Village Voice*, Jacobs honed the ideas that she would set forth in *Death and Life*, as well as the narrative structures and language through which she would articulate those ideas. Even before she started writing *Death and Life*, Jacobs's journalistic form had captured the attention of urban planners and architects. When, prior to awarding Jacobs the Rockefeller Foundation grant, Gilpatric had sought feedback on her proposal from a number of important urban intellectuals, Catherine Bauer encouraged Gilpatric to keep Jacobs from getting "bogged down with academic theorizing or too much would-be-scientific research." The specialist's literary approach, Bauer noted, "isn't her game and she probably knows it, but strange things sometimes happen to good creative popular writers when they get a Foundation grant!" Just as Jacobs envisioned it would be, Bauer recommended to Gilpatric that the book be "sharp and lively *reportage*, for the general public or at least for the 'intelligent interested layman.'"[10] In short, Bauer hoped to see Jacobs approach her book in the same way that she had been writing in newspapers and magazines for years.

The narrative patterns with which Jacobs became familiar as a journalist writing for the general public and as an avid reader of the city's newspapers and magazines shaped the types of stories that she would tell about the city in *Death and Life*. While Jacobs may have been naturally inclined to peer into the city's crevices in order to understand its inner workings, the conventions of urban journalism pushed her to investigate these offbeat locales. She understood what types of stories would appeal to editors and readers. It is difficult to imagine, for instance, that she would have landed four articles in *Vogue* in the mid-1930s as an unknown journalist had she been writing about Wall Street or the Upper West Side. By covering the relatively obscure fur, leather, diamond, and flower districts, Jacobs inserted herself into a long tradition of urban journalism that surveyed the city's foreign territories for readers who might not have been willing to venture into them on their own. Developed by writers such as Charles Dickens and George G. Foster in the mid-19th century, the journalistic sketch had become one of the primary literary forms that urban writers used in order to walk readers through the city's mysterious passages.[11] The opening lines of her sketch about the flower district clearly tap into the tradition established by Dickens and Foster: "All the ingredients of a lavender-and-old-lace story, with a rip-roaring background, are in New York's wholesale flower district, centered around Twenty-Eighth Street and Sixth Avenue. Under the melodramatic roar of the 'El,' encircled by hash-houses in Turkish baths, are the shops of hard-boiled, stalwart men, who shyly admit they are dottles for love, sentiment, and romance."[12] Jacobs's sketch telescopes past the familiar perspective of the El and penetrates the thick skin of the vendors to locate the real life pulsing beneath the surface of the city. Jacobs adopts the persona and literary practices of the beat reporter who scours the city's quirky corners in order to discover and explain "how cities work in real life."[13]

Jacobs may have toned down the geographic sensationalism exhibited in the *Vogue* pieces when writing *Death and Life*, but she continued to activate the narrative conventions of this strain of urban journalism. Even if her intent is ultimately to undermine the logic by which particular urban neighborhoods come to be described as slums and blighted, she nevertheless takes the citizens and laymen who read her book on a slum tour of sorts. Jacobs was just one of many journalists and novelists rushing readers to the "second" ghetto in the 1950s and '60s.[14] She signals her participation in this literary land rush in *Death and Life* by invoking many of the pre- and postwar ghetto's generic landmarks (flophouses, cheap hotels, pawnshops, tattoo parlors, skid rows, housing projects, and turfs) and the urban types that pass through them (juvenile delinquents, hoodlum gangs, bums, immigrants, black migrants, and rats). When Jacobs takes her readers to a public housing project in Brooklyn—where "housing police run up and down" the corridors, elevators, and fire stairs chasing the "malefactors" who "behave barbarously and viciously in the blind-eyed, sixteen-story-high stairways"—her language arouses the type of voyeuristic interest to which journalists and novelists had been catering since the 19th century.[15] Most, though not all, of the time, *Death and Life* strives to unravel the titillating effects that had become bound up with these urban locations and figures. Nevertheless, Jacobs persists in capitalizing on the narrative advantages offered by journalistic sensationalism.

Unlike much of the mid-century literature that explores the city's slums and ghettos, *Death and Life* also takes its middle- and upper-class readers into the kinds of neighborhoods in which they would have been quite comfortable. But even when writing about these more familiar settings, Jacobs defamiliarizes them by making the ordinary exotic. She applies urban journalism's slumming aesthetic to the sidewalks, buildings, and corner stores of places such as Greenwich Village and Philadelphia's Rittenhouse Square. In doing so, *Death and Life* suggests that every part of the city—upper-, middle-, and working-class neighborhoods—is on the verge of becoming a slum. A posh street such as New York's Park Avenue is "so blank of built-in eyes, so devoid of concrete reasons for using or watching it," Jacobs claims, that "if its rents were to slip below the point where they could support a plentiful hired neighborhood of doormen and elevator men, it would undoubtedly become a woefully dangerous street."[16] Jacobs may have imported a narrative template rooted in less affluent urban neighborhoods into more prosperous ones primarily in an attempt to demonstrate that barbarous behavior is not confined to a particular type of urban area, but she also knew that doing so would make for good reading. Readers had long been interested in having exciting vicarious urban experiences, and Jacobs possessed the journalistic writing habits that enabled her to provide them.

Jacobs ratcheted up the popular appeal of *Death and Life* by supplementing the narrative conventions of urban journalism with a distinctly hard-boiled sensibility. It is easy to imagine Jacobs dressed in a trench coat, puffing at her cigarette as she spits out lines such as "Neighborhood is a word that has come to sound like a Valentine."[17] Cultivated in the writings of Dashiell Hammett, Raymond Chandler, and James M. Cain, and further developed through film noir, the hard-boiled voice had become one of the most authoritative for narrating life in the mid-century city. More specifically, though, the hard-boiled genre offered writers a reader-friendly way to talk about the complex social ills of urban life. In these stories, the figure of the gangster or mob boss frequently represents a predatory and monopolistic form of capitalism that threatens to break up an increasingly fragile community. The detective's job is to sort through the shadowy and convoluted urban underworld peopled by gangsters, politicians, and the wealthy in an attempt to defend the powerless.[18] The hard-boiled genre offered Jacobs an ideal boilerplate for narrating the social ills of the urban renewal order. *Death and Life* may lack the narrative suspense of a hard-boiled novel or film, but it utilizes the genre's methods of social diagnosis.

Playing the part of the hard-boiled detective, Jacobs uncovers for readers the sprawling network of urban renewal's corrupt order. Tracing the dispersion of the billions of dollars of "shadow-world money" injected into the city's economy by the federal government, Jacobs makes her way to the pockets of urban planners, *Death and Life*'s equivalent of the hard-boiled gangster's hideout. In their efforts to "house people" in a deliberate and "planned fashion," these planners affix "price tags" to the "population, and each sorted-out chunk of price-tagged populace lives in growing suspicion and tension against the surrounding city." Jacobs accuses urban planners and municipal officials of further eroding the urban community by constructing "[m]onopolistic shopping centers and monumental cultural centers" that mask, "under the public relations hoohaw, the subtraction of commerce, and of culture too, from the intimate and casual life of cities."[19] In Jacobs's telling, urban planners exert the same type of menacing influence over city dwellers as Eddie Mars exercises over the Los Angelenos that populate Raymond Chandler's *The Big Sleep* (1939).

In condemning urban planners for monopolizing control of the urban landscape and thereby fostering suspicion and tension within the city's population, Jacobs fully leverages the diagnostic logic of the hard-boiled genre. If hard-boiled novelists are primarily disturbed by the concentration of capital in the 20th-century city and its effects upon urbanites trying to make an honest living, Jacobs is more particularly troubled by the concentration of the power to shape the built environment that was a consequence of the federal funds that flooded cities such as New York. As much as any gangster or mob boss, urban planners symbolize for Jacobs a threat to the type of urban community that both she and the hard-boiled detective seek to defend. In taking up the role of the detective, Jacobs positions herself as the populist defender not only of "helpless site victims," who are forced to fund their own oppression through taxes, but also of the "[t]housands upon thousands of small businesses" and their "proprietors" that would be "destroyed" and "ruined" by the physical displacements demanded by urban planners, with "hardly a gesture at compensation."[20] Jacobs reasons that, more than even monopolistic capitalists, urban planners interfere with the ability of urbanites to practice the type of small-scale capitalism that lies at the heart of her vision of vital urban communities. Many have rightly criticized Jacobs for placing too much blame upon planners for the city's social problems under the urban renewal order, but her decision to condense these complex problems into a single urban type works really well as a narrative strategy.

## JACOBS'S LITERARY STYLE

If popular urban literary genres provided Jacobs with the narrative hooks that she would use to reel in readers, they also helped her craft a "sharp and lively" voice. Jacobs worked hard to ensure that the more formal aspects of her writing style would be easy on the eyes and ears of her readers. Her experience as a city journalist gave her prose a particularly sharp edge, which can be perceived most clearly when *Death and Life* is read in the context of contemporaneous urban planning literature. Although Jacobs claimed that her manuscript had much in common with Kevin Lynch's *The Image of the City* (1960), the two works provide radically different reading experiences.[21] Lynch's work was, and continues to be, praised by many for its readability, but it is readable in a very different way than *Death and Life*. The following sentence typifies Lynch's style: "But let the mishap of disorientation once occur, and the sense of anxiety and even terror that accompanies it reveals to us how closely it is linked to our sense of balance and well-being." Despite his attempt to achieve a "speculative" and slightly "irresponsible" tone in his writing, Lynch couldn't quite shake the formal and scientific trappings of the large research university in which he worked.[22] *The Image of the City* may deliver great insights into the sensuous experience of living in and moving through the urban environment, but its prose ultimately places readers in an MIT lecture hall. Lynch's description of getting lost in the city—"the mishap of disorientation"—conjures the voice of a tweed-jacketed professor speaking in an affected accent. Like many other urban planners and architects who wrote about the city's built environment, Lynch's diction, sentence structure, and even layout are tethered to the conventions of academic writing.

Jacobs frequently expressed her distaste for the academy and strove to distance herself from its stranglehold on the literature of urban planning. She achieved this distance by forging her own literary style in several of the city's journalistic venues. The opening of her *Vogue* article on the flower district exhibits one of Jacobs's most distinct stylistic traits: hyphenation. Her propensity to cobble together words with hyphens, while not necessarily typical of urban journalism, typifies Jacobs's way with language. The hyphenated phrases sprinkled into the *Vogue* piece—"lavender-and-old-lace story," "rip-roaring background"—flood the prose of *Death and Life*: "close-grained diversity," "heart-of-the-day ballet," "hop-and-skip relationships," "border-prone territories," "sorted-out sets of statistics."[23] These moments of hyphenation clearly mark Jacobs's refusal to get bogged down in the academic and scientific discourse of urban planning. In most cases, she could have easily substituted a single word for those she strung together with hyphens, but doing so would have required her to dip into the specialist's glossary. Jacobs's commitment to user-friendly diction also results in many of the book's other linguistic peculiarities. The hyphen can be seen as the stylistic sibling of what many have described as Jacobs's folksy language—her unabashed use of colloquialisms ("Handsome is as handsome does") and slang ("hoohaw").[24]

If the hyphen gave Jacobs a way to show her intellectual solidarity with the general public, she also used it to signal her commitment to a writing style that honors the spoken word. Jacobs cared immensely about how her language felt in the mouths and sounded in the ears of her readers. It is not difficult to imagine her talking through sentences out loud in her writing studio before typing them. In Jacobs's hands, the hyphen became a particularly effective tool for amplifying the sound of the written word. It gave her more flexibility to establish rhythm ("hop-and-skip relationships"), to rhyme ("heart-of-the-day ballet"), and to alliterate ("sorted-out sets of statistics"). Jacobs reinforced the auditory effects that she achieved with hyphenated language at nearly every turn. Hyphen or no hyphen, she was a sucker for alliteration. On a single page of *Death and Life*, she commits at least five blatant alliterative acts: "vapid vulgarity," "standardized suburban chain-store shopping," "sacking of cities," "prove even poorer than their poor pretenses," and my personal favorite, "galloping gangrene."[25] Jacobs was an equally inveterate italicizer and capitalizer. Where most writers italicize as a way to heighten the significance of a particular word or phrase, Jacobs uses italics primarily as a way to indicate vocal fluctuation: "[Planners and architects] have gone to great pains to learn what the saints and sages of modern orthodox planning have said about how cities *ought* to work and what *ought* to be good for people and businesses in them." Jacobs also capitalizes phrases normally undeserving of such an honor, to similar vocal effect: "Radiant Garden City Beautiful," "Great Blight of Dullness," "This is City Planning," "More Open Space."[26] Through these and a variety of other literary strategies, she entices readers to vocalize the words on the page. Her prose pulls readers out of the silence of the private reading act and situates them in an interpersonal exchange in which language remains inextricably linked to its sounds.

*Death and Life*'s strong aural notes point to a past in which Jacobs's vocal resistance to urban redevelopment at professional conferences, community forums, and impromptu rallies often found their way into print. Her career-making speech at the 1956 Harvard Urban Design Conference, for instance, appeared shortly thereafter as an article in *Architectural Forum*.[27] In 1957, the *Village Voice* reprinted the complete transcript of a speech that she had delivered at the concluding Cooper Union Forum on the problems facing Greenwich Village. Reading these vocal performances in print illuminates the extent to which Jacobs's writing practices were rooted in an urban oral tradition. These spoken-written hybrids suggest that Jacobs wrote *Death and Life* in much the same way that she prepared her speeches. She begins her address to the audience at the Cooper Union Forum with the type of analogy that she employs throughout *Death and Life*. Hoping to convince the audience of the absurdity of the city's proposal to construct a four-lane highway through Washington Square Park, she tells the crowd a story about a man who, seeking a cure for his cold, is instructed by his doctor: "'Go home, put up the window, lie down with your pajamas open, and let the wind run through.' 'But doctor,' said the man, 'I might get pneumonia!' 'Exactly,' said the doctor, glancing at his aureomycin: 'We know how to cure that!'" Jacobs quickly and straightforwardly transposes the story into a register that clarifies its relevance for her listeners: "This is very much like the case of Greenwich Village. Here is the Village, conferring with Drs. Wiley and Moses. 'I tell you what,' says Dr. Wiley, 'Go home, lay down your park, open it up and let the traffic rush through.' 'But doctor,' says the Village, 'I might get Blight!' 'Exactly,' chimes in Dr. Moses, glancing at his bulldozer: 'We know how to cure that!'"[28] This particular analogy stands as both a stylistic and a topical precursor to *Death and Life*'s arresting comparison of the field of urban planning to the practice of bloodletting. "As in the pseudoscience of bloodletting," Jacobs explains, "just so in the pseudoscience of city rebuilding and planning, years of learning and a plethora of subtle and complicated dogma have arisen on a foundation of nonsense."[29] By repeatedly utilizing this particular figure of speech in *Death and Life*, Jacobs recreates for her readers the atmosphere of the public gathering.

When reading *Death and Life* it often feels as if Jacobs transcribed entire passages from a political rally or street-corner sermon, because, in fact, she often had. Given that Jacobs discovered part of her urban voice as a community activist in the city's streets, parks, and meeting halls, it makes sense that her writing reenacts for readers the experience of being in public with strangers. Jacobs never strikes an intimate tone. Reading *Death and Life* is not like having a private, one-on-one conversation peppered with inside jokes but more like striking up a conversation with someone on the street. *Death and Life* reenacts its definition of the city as a place of casual public contact in its very form and style. Rather than resurrect voices from formal surveys, Jacobs litters her text with voices from, and conversations that took place on, the sidewalk, in bars, or on public telephones—a stylistic strategy that Jacobs may have picked up from the many settlement-house workers with whom she associated. We constantly witness Jacobs "getting in on some talk." Much like the settlement studies that Jacobs quotes throughout *Death and Life*, her own study encourages readers to think of the city as a stage for innumerable little "sidewalk contacts" rather than as a backdrop for intimate relationships.[30] Her literary style reinforces her argument that healthy urban spaces exert a strong pull upon their inhabitants to engage with one another. In her estimation, it requires effort to be isolated and alienated. One must resist the temptation to engage in conversation. Jacobs's analogies, metaphors, and other forms of figurative speech re-create the social space of the city sidewalk, within which a diverse body of readers can gather without having to disclose personal matters.

Jacobs's somewhat flamboyant attempts to draw out the oral nature of language do not carve out an obvious place for her within the tradition of mainstream journalism, whose touchstones are objective observations and neutral language. Her journalistic pedigree connects her instead to an alternative family of reporters and writers. Charles Abrams was on the right track when, shortly after the publication of *Death and Life*, he remarked somewhat offhandedly that Jacobs had "come to the big city's defense with an exposition that would make E. B. White, O. Henry, and Meyer Berger forever sing her praises."[31] Although she never published anything in the *New Yorker*, Jacobs practiced a form of urban journalism that had been nurtured more deliberately in its pages than in any other publication. In addition to White and Berger, writers such as Joseph Mitchell and A. J. Liebling led the charge in developing journalistic forms and styles that sought to capture the highly interconnected nature of urban life. *New Yorker* writers taught their readers to perceive and recognize the value of the social interconnections in which they were already and inevitably enmeshed. Taking her cues from this variety of urban journalists, Jacobs found venues in which she could experiment with style and make her own contributions to this particular strain of city journalism.

## FROM JOURNALIST TO AUTHOR

Jacobs's journalism experience certainly helped make *Death and Life* as appealing and readable as it is, but her years of writing and editing for newspapers and magazines presented several compositional challenges as she worked on her first book-length manuscript. When Jacobs wrote Gilpatric in the summer of 1959 to request the additional funding from the Rockefeller Foundation, she also took the opportunity to share why progress on the manuscript had been a bit slow. "Never having attempted to write a book of this sort before," she explained, "I did not anticipate the difficulties I was going to get into in organizing and writing." Before she had even begun the writing project that would become *Death and Life*, Jacobs had debated whether to write a series of short articles or take on an entire book. Although she knew up front that writing a book would be "far different from writing and organizing articles," she admitted to Gilpatric that she had "no conception" of how different executing the two genres would be until she finally "waded in." She continued, "In retrospect, how overoptimistic I was about the writing!" Jacobs closed her letter by assuring Gilpatric that she had, "through considerable trial, error and bafflement," worked through her organizational issues.[32]

It is debatable, in the end, whether or not Jacobs made the transition from composing short articles to writing a book as successfully as she had hoped she would. Some of the persisting trouble may have had to do with the tall and complex organizational task that Jacobs had given herself. In writing *Death and Life*, she was, as she informed Gilpatric, attempting to work out in book form "what amounts to a different system of thought about the great city." Communicating this new system of thought would require showing readers the complex interrelations of the city's many relatively simple parts: sidewalks, parks, neighborhoods, and so on. Jacobs acknowledged that the "organization of this complexity without confusion is not like chopping off blocks of wood: there, that one's done, now for the next." Instead, revealing the complexity of these urban interrelations requires that the "logic of every part is a portion of the logic of the whole, done in the light of the whole."[33] In my reading of *Death and Life*, the book falls short of establishing a memorable, coherent, and overarching whole into which I can mentally slot each individual section. If the episodic nature of the book underscores Jacobs's belief in the power of small-scale, casual interactions among urbanites, it simultaneously interferes with an ability to grasp the new system of thought that she intended to communicate. When in the thick of Jacobs's close readings of particular urban forms, it is easy to forget how her assessment of each urban part contributes to the book's larger argument. As a result, reading *Death and Life* can feel, at times, like reading a series of sketches or short articles.

Although her subsequent books failed to match *Death and Life*'s popular appeal, Jacobs addressed many of its structural shortcomings in these later works. *Death and Life* marked a transition in Jacobs's career from writing newspaper and magazine articles to writing books. She may have spun off magazine articles from these book manuscripts, but these later projects were conceived from their inception—and generally behaved—as books. As she continued to work with this particular literary form, Jacobs mastered its narrative conventions and achieved the type of structural coherence that *Death and Life* had not quite obtained. Written in the same journalistic style and tone as *Death and Life*, *The Economy of Cities* (1969) and *Cities and the Wealth of Nations* (1984) provide a more fluid reading experience from start to finish. In these books, the reader can more easily grasp the way in which the "logic of every part is a portion of the logic of the whole." In *Systems of Survival* (1992) and *The Nature of Economies* (2000), Jacobs departed from the conventional journalism she had been writing for nearly six decades, experimenting instead with the "venerable literary form" of "imaginary characters and didactic dialogue." Her adoption of this literary form would, Jacobs hoped, invite readers to "join the characters and enter the argument too"—to collaborate in the production of, rather than consume, meaning.[34] These more experimental works reveal Jacobs's ongoing attempts to ensure that the form of her writing gives readers unobstructed access to its message and serve as a reminder of her dedication to her craft as a writer. Jacobs thought of herself as an author to the end.

If there is a lesson to be learned from Jacobs by those whose business it is to write about architecture and city planning, it is that we ought to be more open to learning from others whose business it is to write for the general public. This lesson, for some reason, has been hard to grasp. Many of *Death and Life*'s early readers, in fact, fretted over Jacobs's popular and accessible style. In his review of *Death and Life* for the newsletter of the American Society of Planning Officials—one of the American Planning Association's parent organizations—Dennis O'Harrow praised Jacobs for making urban planning, a "subject that is normally somewhat dull (in the eyes of the public)," a subject that is "reasonably readable." While O'Harrow's instincts told him that this was a good thing—that planning literature ought to be somewhat enjoyable—his professional training caused him to be suspicious of Jacobs's talent for appealing "to the reader through his emotions." O'Harrow worried that her emotionally charged book would be "grabbed by screwballs and reactionaries and used to fight civic improvement and urban renewal projects for years to come."[35] Depending on whom you talk to, O'Harrow's worst fears may or may not have come to pass. However, most people now agree that *Death and Life* is more than just "reasonably readable" and that Jacobs's writing style is to be emulated rather than shunned. She teaches all of us who write about the city's built and social environment the importance of looking to, and perhaps even aspiring to become, "good creative popular writers."

# URBAN WARFARE:
# THE BATTLES FOR BUENOS AIRES

## SERGIO KIERNAN

In 2009 there was a rebellion in the San Telmo neighborhood of Buenos Aires, Argentina. An old working-class area not far from the central business district, San Telmo was the first preservation area in Argentina and is now very popular with tourists. Longtime residents have seen the traditional shops vanish, industrial uses and workshops reduced to a goldsmith and an upscale framer, and the storefronts taken up with antiques shops and expensive bars. Gentrification long ago eliminated flophouses and cheap housing, turning tenements into loft and studio units. The main thoroughfare, Defensa Street, becomes a pedestrian mall every weekend, with musicians, peddlers, and mimes plying their trades.

When the city government decided to turn Defensa Street into a permanent pedestrian mall, San Telmo exploded in demonstrations, sit-ins, and neighbors' meetings. It was an uncommon situation: a community mobilized to stop, rather than demand, a public works project supposedly designed for their benefit. The city's minister of urban development grudgingly had to accept a public audience to explain the work to the neighbors. There he presented a whole battery of PowerPoint presentations and renderings showing smiling residents and tourists walking along a renovated Defensa Street. Then the residents took the floor and gave the minister a piece of their mind.

It felt very much the way it must have in Greenwich Village in the 1950s during the debates over highways and urban overpasses: a wave of common sense hitting a wall of architectural conventional wisdom. The residents spoke of mixed uses, of the vitality of a street, of security, of the effects of too much specialization in an area. They complained that the plans to so radically change Defensa implied a loss of public transportation, and said that while the mall would perhaps be popular with tourists, it would certainly be a hit with the homeless. And they made it absolutely clear to the officials that they hated the idea of turning their homes into a tourist attraction.

San Telmo is far from New York City, but its inhabitants were using arguments straight from Jane Jacobs: the uses of sidewalks, the importance of diversity, the risk of the district's self-destruction, the power of gentrification. Nobody at the meeting had ever heard of Jacobs, and they were amazed and happy to hear from me that long ago an author had analyzed the life of cities in a way so close to their agenda.[1] The officials—all architects—had vaguely heard of her work, and they were not too happy to hear of it again.

Part of their discomfort arose from the similarities between the New York City Jacobs wrote about and the Buenos Aires of today. Both cities were effectively created by immigrants, starting out as rather small colonial villages; and both adopted, with élan and a happy abandon, all kinds of architectural styles. Colonial Buenos Aires was a very minor port where people made a living by smuggling and by supplying goods and services to passing fleets. Far from "real" cities—such as Lima, Peru; Mexico City; and Havana, Cuba—it was an end of the line for the Spanish Empire, important only as an outpost against the encroaching Portuguese. Independence was kind to Argentina and its capital city, and by the late 19th century Buenos Aires was booming and had become the second-largest immigration port in the Americas after New York.

The city these immigrants built was well planned and open, with wide avenues and the Spanish-style grid broken by boulevards. Downtown was the place for tall buildings, while outlying neighborhoods—connected to the center by tramways, urban railroads, and buses—had their own smaller shopping and entertainment districts. The quality of building was remarkable; public buildings were erected in the grandest French styles, in stark contrast with the humble adobes of the colonial era. Private citizens followed the example, creating thousands of homes, large and small, in the best Italian, French, and English styles, with a bit of German and Eastern European for flavor. Being a success story in Buenos Aires meant moving into a house with Carrara marble steps, French ironwork in the window frames, stained-glass windows imported from Germany, and Slovenian oak flooring. A city of 3 million people was created out of a village in just 40 years. This massive building project created one very large and fine collection of architectural landmarks, and a very high quality of life for residents. To this day, Buenos Aires is the safest, most livable city of its size in South America, with areas of great beauty and large parks.

Then three factors intervened. By the late 1950s, political instability had destroyed what had been the eighth-highest per-capita income in the world: Argentina became poorer. At the same time, the city was filled to its limits, and the only way to build the new was to destroy the old, replacing smaller buildings with high rises. The third factor was the explosion of a commercial architecture totally indifferent to any public responsibility or aesthetic criteria. This was a deep change in the building industry, which from then on looked for profit and profit alone. Half a century later, the average new building in Buenos Aires is a squarish high rise of reinforced concrete, with walls made with the cheapest available bricks, second-rate metal windows, and artificial wood doors. Very rarely is a creative impulse to be seen. Urban density has gone up. Formerly quiet neighborhoods have become masses of 10- or 11-story buildings that are hard to tell apart. There are cars everywhere, since they have become cheaper, and quiet and safe streets where children could play are a nostalgic memory.

By the early 21st century, the situation had become untenable. The building boom accelerated after the bust and recession of 2001–2002, as developers profited from new regulations that permitted them to build higher and consolidate plots in order to construct skyscrapers. New zoning regulations were passed that favored the biggest developers, and for the first time in its history Buenos Aires had buildings of 40 stories and more. The *porteños*, as locals are called, saw with stark clarity that their future might very well include living in urban desolation such as that in Mexico City and São Paulo, Brazil—cities famous for crime, pollution, and alienation. A countermovement arose, with NGOs being created all over the city; many of them published manifestos that Jacobs would likely have signed. The mystery is how her ideas became so common on the South American continent.

Only two of Jane Jacobs's books were ever translated into Spanish, and that was decades ago. One has to dig deep and search wide to find somebody who actually remembers her name, has found it in a bibliography, or had to read her work to prepare for a test. Still, her idea of what a city is, how it should be thought out, and how fragile an instrument it is seems to be firmly rooted in South America. Just as few people actually undergo psychoanalysis but almost everybody knows that there is an id, Jacobs's concepts of what makes a street livable, why projects do not work, and how social engineering is a recipe for trouble are current in the lively debate over cities in South America even though few people have studied her work. Whether in relation to the violence of Ciudad Juárez, Mexico, the gigantism of São Paulo, the rapid decline of Lima, or the excessive vitality of Buenos Aires, Jacobs is part of the debate.

Brazilians have always had to read Jacobs either in English or Spanish, for none of her books has ever been translated into Portuguese. *The Death and Life of Great American Cities* was published in Spain in 1967 and reprinted in 1973. In 1971 there was a Spanish edition of *The Economy of Cities*.[2] That's the sum total of Jacobs's bibliography in Spanish, still circulating in tattered, 40-year-old paperbacks. The copies are hard to come by: There is one in the vaults of the Central Society of Architects in Buenos Aires, where the librarians keep the less popular books, and nobody has asked to see it since the 1990s. Some architects and many urban planners treasure their copies. One can find copies in English in private collections and at the School of Design of the Universidad Torcuato Di Tella in Buenos Aires.

In part, Jacobs's ideas circulate among professionals in the form of reading assignments for students and quotes by teachers and authors. In 2010, her work was assigned to students in Córdoba, Argentina; Madrid, Spain; and Santa Catarina, Brazil.[3] Blogs and e-zines play a wide role in introducing Jacobs to a professional audience: *Arqa*, *El Malpensante*, and *Nomada* are among the ones that quote her work the most.[4] Those blogs link readers to sites such as the Project for Public Spaces and to booksellers offering copies of Jacobs's books in English, and they publish Spanish and Spanish-speaking authors' writings on Jacobs.

What Latin American readers find in Jacobs are solutions. A young mid-ranking official in the Buenos Aires city government recalled for me his first contact with her work. A decade ago, while working on a postgraduate degree in urban economy at the Di Tella University, he found a copy in English of *Death and Life* at the library. "It was a revelation, to find systematized many things that you think and feel, rendered in such a simple language. I took away some very strong ideas that I use—or try to use—in my work as an official: that streets and urban spaces are not an issue for professionals only, that the quality of life in a city depends more on its people than on its architecture, that officials should be aware that they are there to help the people revitalize and maintain their neighborhoods and not to tell them what to do."

This official—who has run into much trouble with colleagues and superiors over public management models—was actively involved in a project to limit outdoor advertising in Buenos Aires. "We were looking for equilibrium between commercial and residential uses," he said. "We understood that an excess of advertisement is, in Jacobsian terms, a threat to diversity." He believes that it "can and will destroy the formula that makes for a lively neighborhood," signifying overspecialization and degrading the appearance of an area.

Another instance of a Jacobsian influence is the nascent legal arguments neighborhood associations are using to try to stop overdevelopment in many cities across the continent. The "quality of life" argument, as it's come to be known, starts with the idea that there is an implicit contract between officials and residents when it comes to zoning: Neighborhoods are collective creations that were actively shaped by their inhabitants or were chosen by them because of their characteristics. People who moved into a low-density area with small shops and quiet streets did not do so expecting future high-rise development. They opted for more sunlight and peace and quiet, and accepted the downsides: lack of amenities, less transportation. Officials should not impose "progress" on those communities.[5] The opening of a major shopping center—the Dot Baires mall—in a formerly very quiet neighborhood in December 2009 created a legal battle that the neighbors lost. City Hall permitted the building of the massive mall with no regard to transit and safety problems, using two arguments: Private property cannot be limited, and a mall is intrinsically a sign of progress in a "stagnant" area.

A longer legal battle took place in 2010 over the building of a 40-story building on Garay Avenue, right on the edge of the San Telmo preservation area and smack in the middle of a neighborhood where the highest building was a little more than 40 feet. Local NGOs asked for help from Basta de Demoler, a fast-growing NGO that managed to change the map of preservation in Buenos Aires with a legal case in 2008.[6] Late in 2009, the San Telmo residents and Basta de Demoler filed for a stay of action at the building site. The developers appealed, and work started—but Basta de Demoler appealed and got a new stay. The huge building project was paralyzed for six months, while the courts examined the case and City Hall tried to convince the developers to change their design and build something wider and less tall (they refused). In October 2010, the court permitted the developers to finish their building, but only because the law, as it stood, did not provide the executive with tools to preserve the quality of life of the neighborhood. With a degree of sincerity rarely seen in legal proceedings, the judges said that the residents were right but they couldn't stop the developers.

A striking characteristic of these stories is how widely they were covered by the media, which has found a new villain in developers. In September 2010 a building site in Villa Pueyrredón, a nice middle-class area of Buenos Aires, was the scene of a grave accident. A developer, building yet another high rise, failed to reinforce the sides of the excavations for foundations. Early one evening, a mechanical digger went a foot too far under the foundations of the neighboring three-story 1930s French-style building, which housed shops, apartments, and a gym. The building collapsed, three young customers of the gym died, and 10 others were hurt. The reaction was enormous: hours of live coverage, reams of editorial comment, a general condemnation of the developers, and denunciations of the lack of public controls. City government was thrown on the defensive, took away the licenses of all professionals involved, and triggered a wave of inspections at other building sites.[7]

By late 2010, the city's government had a crisis on its hands. The city's governor is a civil engineer, and all officials involved in public spaces, licensing, supervision, and control—down to the level of assistant secretary and general director—are engineers or architects.[8] After campaigning in 2007 as an expert in cities and buildings, Governor Mauricio Macri can hardly claim ignorance of the situation. His three years in office have shown him—along with close political allies and officials in his cabinet such as Daniel Chain and Hector Lostri, both architects—to be a creative enemy of landmarking, preservation, and the efforts to limit density in residential neighborhoods.

Their most Machiavellian move was to turn around a small institution that the city legislature had given permitting authority for the demolition of older buildings. In late 2008, the legislature approved a law creating a special procedure to protect all buildings erected before 1940. The admittedly arbitrary date was set because in that year an aerial survey of Buenos Aires was carried out, providing a detailed snapshot of the city with its traditional buildings in place. The legislature mandated that the little-known Advisory Council on Landmarks was to become a filter for demolition permits involving those buildings. Every developer's proposal to destroy a building of any kind built before January 1, 1941, had to be vetted by the council. If the council found no merit in the building, the permit was issued straightaway, but if it found architectural or historical value in it, the file would be sent to the legislature, which would consider the building for landmarking.

Of course, a government so intimately connected with the building industry could not fail to see the risk for developers: They no longer knew where to buy property to demolish and build, and it could take legislators years to make a decision on a development proposal. In short, there was no way to set a price for older, smaller buildings in areas where developers wanted to build high rises.

The "solution" to the problem was indeed concise. The council suddenly started considering every building built before 1941 plus its "immediate environment," curiously defined as the block where it stood and not the block frontage across the street. What that created was an instant database of building sites, hundreds of houses that could legally be destroyed, a guarantee that there would be no hurdles. The results were so slanted that the council is approving for demolition 11 sites for every one it sends to the legislature to be considered for preservation. The council, made up mostly of public officials, proved pliable and sensitive to the political priorities of the city's administration.

As of this writing, the battle is on. Residents are growing more confident about trying to limit the sway of officials and are creating a new language to attempt to preserve their city from unwanted developers. They are not concerned with train stations, public buildings, and large private residences that have already been preserved as landmarks. Their aim is to stop the destruction of whole neighborhoods where single-family houses and other small buildings are being replaced by buildings between eight and 11 stories high. Their foremost complaints are the shoddy quality of new buildings and, more important, the decrease in the quality of life in close-knit communities that they say are being tinkered with by parties interested only in making money. That's very much an argument in Jacobsian terms, and it will be highly interesting to see her ideas about urban life applied to shantytowns and informal settlements, and gentrified and gentrifying areas such as Palermo Viejo and Barracas. That her ideas travel so well is a compliment to the robust common sense that was central to her work.

It is encouraging that politicians—*even* politicians, it could be said—are taking up the issue. In October 2010, three laws were tabled in the city assembly to reform the Advisory Council on Landmarks, curtailing its powers to approve buildings for demolition and making it mandatory that NGOs and preservation institutions have seats and votes on the council. These laws differed only in details and received support from most parties represented in the assembly, the ruling Propuesta Republicana (PRO) included. At the same time, two other initiatives were suggested, one to rezone a vast area on the south side of Buenos Aires, the other to introduce penalties for developers that destroy landmarked buildings. Both future laws will make it expensive for developers to break the law and less profitable for them to demolish and rebuild in protected areas.

This trend could provide preservation regulations with teeth. No Buenos Aires city government ever invested in a real enforcement capability, and fines are laughably small. But developers have to respect the building code at the very basic level of a building's footprint and height, since it's very hard to hide extra stories or greater width. Since the only current penalty for demolishing a landmarked building is a limitation on future square footage—70 percent of the destroyed surface as the upper limit—enforcement is possible at the permits stage. This penalty is rarely applied since city government has not felt any pressure to enforce the rules. A second option discussed by assembly members is the English model: reconstruction of the destroyed building using period materials.

The simple fact that such utopias are being considered, and potential votes in their favor can be counted on, are signs of the times. The tide might be turning in Buenos Aires.

# THE MAGPIE AND THE BEE:

## JANE JACOBS'S MAGNIFICENT OBSESSION

### RICHARD HARRIS

Nineteen sixty-one was a vintage year. Jane Jacobs published her first, enormously influential, book about cities, and E. H. Carr produced a wonderful account of the writing of good nonfiction. Better still, they connect.

In *What Is History?* Carr speaks as a historian, but much of what he says can be generalized. Early on, he tackles the question of what the proper relationship is between the writer and his or her facts. Dismissing the suggestion that facts speak for themselves, he points out that writers select particular information to buttress their arguments. He goes on to advise the novice reader to listen for the "buzzing" of ideas. If you cannot hear any, he suggests, either you are tone deaf or the author is a "dull dog."[1]

Whatever her limitations as a writer—and I will speak of some—Jane Jacobs was never dull. Her works buzz with ideas that distill the hum of the city. She always had a bee in her bonnet, a term she herself used in print on several occasions. She tore into a certain variety of planner, lovingly evoked street life, praised small-scale diversity, grew passionate about all forms of creativity, and above all defended cities. She did not equivocate; in her writing, as in her community politics, she takes no prisoners; she isn't subtle or shy. Her arguments are clearly stated; her obsession with the city is there for all to see. Today, even tone-deaf readers cannot miss her message.

If Jane Jacobs can be likened to any creature, it is surely the magpie. This bird is notorious for selecting flashy items with which to decorate its nest. There is no better analogy for the way that Jacobs gets her reader's attention by displaying anecdotes. Like the magpie with its pieces of candy wrapper, Jacobs uses her illustrations to complete an edifice, which in her case, I will argue, is a theory of how cities matter. The comparison can be taken further.

Although the magpie presumably thinks of its nest as one entity, ornithologists view it as having two sections, a base and a roof. So, too, although Jacobs's books about cities arguably form a connected whole, they have usually been treated as separate entities. They have influenced different groups of people, whose use of them has been selective and largely nonoverlapping. Rather than perpetuate this selectivity, I will here outline what I see as the major continuities across Jacobs's writings. These are defined by her magnificent obsession—the city—and by her conviction that cities have always mattered, especially because of their built form. She explored the social and economic aspects of this insight at different scales, and presented her conclusions so systematically that they amount to a theory of the significance of urban form. I will argue then that, contrary to a common perception, Jacobs's purpose was largely theoretical. It is in this light that the unitary character of her writings about cities should be viewed.

## A Growing and Diverse Influence

Readers of this book do not need to be told that Jane Jacobs has had a huge influence on the way scholars and planners think about cities. What they may not appreciate is the timing and nature of that influence, and these details matter.

Jacobs made a name for herself as an activist and writer in the late 1950s and early 1960s, notably with *The Death and Life of Great American Cities* (1961).[2] This book immediately drew attention. It received some criticism but widespread praise, and within a decade it had been extensively used and cited by those who opposed modernist-style urban renewal. Its influence is well known and can be quantified by counting how often it has been cited in the journals included in the Web of Science database.[3] By the late 1960s, *Death and Life* was receiving about 20 academic citations annually. Based on this indicator, its influence remained more or less steady for two decades, growing a little in the late 1970s, then waning slightly in the 1980s. In the mid-1990s, it took off. Annual citations jumped from about 30 in the mid-1990s to 80 in the early 2000s and reached 120 in 2008–2009. This corresponds to the emergence of interest in new urbanism, a movement that owes something to Jacobs's ideas and that has helped stimulate interest in them. What is interesting is that a parallel trend is apparent for Jacobs's second-most-influential book, *The Economy of Cities* (1969). Although its citations have always been fewer, lately their rate of growth has been equally steep.

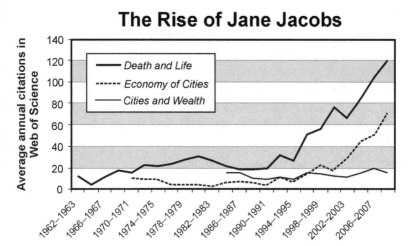

## The Rise of Jane Jacobs

Since she delighted in thinking by analogy, Jacobs might have noted that the trend lines for citations of her works are similar to those that tracked house prices before the bubble burst in 2007–2008. The comparison should not be overdrawn—between 1995 and 2009, the number of citations of urban topics increased almost as rapidly as those of Jacobs's work—but it is not entirely fanciful. During property booms, everyone tries to jump on the bandwagon, while naysayers are drowned out. So, too, among Jacobsians. To be sure, Jacobs has always had her academic critics: Notably, Lewis Mumford and Herbert Gans both expressed significant reservations in early reviews of *Death and Life*. Ever since, there have always been those who deplore Jacobs's lack of rigor, her reliance on anecdotal examples, her inconsistency in citing sources, and her apparently cavalier approach to research. There are even signs that, following a period of respectful silence following her death in 2006, criticism is becoming more pointed and more common. Benjamin Schwarz's 2010 article in the *Atlantic* is a straw in the wind. But the critics are still not very vocal, and her press is overwhelmingly favorable. It is difficult to find a sustained criticism, still less a critique, of her work. This is troublesome: Uncritical praise is unhelpful. But bubble or not, the influence of Jacobs's ideas has certainly boomed in the past decade. She has never been more influential.[4]

While the academic profile of Jacobs's body of work has risen, few writers see it as an intellectually coherent whole. Urbanists have fastened on specific ideas as expressed in one book, and ignored others. In particular, those inspired by *Death and Life* ignore *The Economy of Cities*, and vice versa, a division that corresponds, respectively, with those who are interested in the social life and economic dynamics of cities. *Death and Life* is, above all, about everyday life in the city and how to foster it. As Roger Montgomery once observed, although Jacobs framed it as a critique of planners, it was really a paean to diverse neighborhoods. It is this quality that continues to inspire those who are interested in understanding or fostering vibrant districts.[5] In the Web of Science, journals are grouped into broad categories. Since 1975, those in which *Death and Life* has been cited fall mostly into the broad categories of urban studies (32 percent) and environmental studies (21 percent), and then more focused fields, with economics (4.5 percent) trailing in eighth place. In contrast, journals in the field of economics rank first (38 percent) as sources of citations of *The Economy of Cities*, which is concerned above all with what makes cities economically dynamic.[6] An intermediate pattern of citation is apparent for *Cities and the Wealth of Nations* (1984), the third and by far least influential book in Jacobs's urban trilogy. Overall, then, these three books have attracted very different audiences.

It is not surprising that different researchers have found inspiration in different works. After all, why should *Handbook of Regional and Urban Economics*, which indexes 11 references to *The Economy of Cities*, also take note of *Death and Life*?[7] Still, it is more striking and significant that so few bridge these concerns, making use of both *Death and Life* and one of the other works. In the edited collection *Block by Block: Jane Jacobs and the Future of New York* (2007), for example, most of the 43 contributors speak to local neighborhood and planning issues; only four, including a cartoonist, refer to the economic significance of cities.[8] A similar type of emphasis on one aspect or another of Jacobs's work is generally apparent. An analysis of the Web of Science database in mid-2010 showed that of the 200 most recently published articles citing *Death and Life*, only 10 also refer to *The Economy of Cities*.[9] Moreover, on closer inspection, it turns out that among these 10 only four make nontrivial use of the ideas in both books.[10] Overlaps between *Death and Life* and *Cities and Wealth* (two out of 200) are fewer still, although, as one might expect, those between *The Economy of Cities* and *Cities and Wealth* (22 out of 200) are quite substantial. These findings show that Jacobs's writings about cities have influenced at least two quite distinct groups of researchers, each of whose perception of her work is substantially incomplete.

But perhaps the way researchers have used Jacobs's writings is reasonable: Her writings are diverse, so maybe they need not be seen as a whole. Clearly, each of these three books does focus on a different question: What makes cities worth living in? What makes them economically dynamic? How do they contribute to economic growth? But I believe that the ways Jacobs frames, addresses, and answers those questions have enough in common to justify seeing her body of work on cities as a connected whole.

## A CONSISTENT METHOD

Famously, in the concluding chapter of *Death and Life*, Jacobs asks what "kind of problem the city is." To make sense of her answer, we need to consider what kind of thinker she was.

The conventional wisdom, fostered by Jacobs herself, is that she worked inductively and was averse to theory. This is a quarter truth. Far from being averse to theory, she devoted most of her life to developing it. All her major works are guided by clear questions and a theoretical purpose. As a result, they take a logically structured form. This is most obviously true of *Cities and Wealth*, which explains economic growth through a systematic treatment of cities and regions at different scales; the significance of innovation, technology, and capital; and the contrasting dynamics of growth and decline. Jacobs takes almost as systematic an approach in *The Economy of Cities*, which was her personal favorite and is in my view her most persuasive work because it is the most consistently plausible. Notably, she provides a quasi-mathematical appendix that includes diagrammatic analyses of the key mechanisms of "export generation" and "import replacement." But *Death and Life*, too, was systematically designed to introduce and justify "new principles of city planning and rebuilding." The major sections deal in turn with "the peculiar nature of cities," "the conditions for city diversity," "the forces of decline and regeneration," and "tactics" for revival. For this reason, Peter Laurence has claimed that "Jacobs was also a theorist." I would suggest that "also" understates the point. Pierre Desrochers and Gert-Jan Hospers seem to arrive at this conclusion in the course of their assessment of Jacobs's contribution to economic theory. Noting that "she always rejected all ideologies and labels," they add that "she strived to develop a coherent framework of her own" and produced "a complex theoretical framework." In fact, the production of such a framework was her main, and consistent, purpose. At the end of the first paragraph of *The Economy of Cities*, Jacobs herself speaks frankly of her "effort to develop a theory of city economic growth." What could be clearer? That is why it was plausible for Robert Lucas, himself a Nobel prizewinner in economics, to lobby the prize committee on Jacobs's behalf, citing her contribution to economic theory. More generally, one of the main reasons why Jacobs has been so influential is that big ideas frame all of her key works. These can be pithily expressed: "the ballet of the sidewalks," "the valuable impracticalities of cities," and so forth. Far from being averse to theory, then, she was driven by the desire to create it. Like many theorists, of course, she had a strong preference for her own homegrown variety.[11] What makes her truly distinctive is that she so rarely felt the need to define her own ideas explicitly and consistently in relation to those of other theorists. Rather than upgrade or extend an existing idea, or work within an established grid of assumptions, she preferred to bulldoze everything and start from scratch. There are curious parallels between her approach and that adopted by those advocates of old-style urban renewal whom she so vigorously criticized.

The other, and this time half-plausible, part of the usual view of her research is that she worked inductively. The best, although brief, published statement of her procedure occurs in a letter she wrote that Richard Keeley quoted in his assessment of her work. On the subject of how she had worked in the 1970s and 1980s, Jacobs writes, "I read as omnivorously as I can manage, in anything that interests me. I often don't even know why I'm interested in some facet . . . [but] I've learned to trust myself." At some point in the process, she suggests, patterns began to "show up of their own accord, just out of the material itself." It seems that there could hardly be a clearer statement, or example, of the inductive method. And by all accounts, the manner in which she arrived at the ideas that informed her early work, notably *Death and Life*, was similar. The only difference is that in this work she relied on personal observation, as with her celebrated description of the sidewalk ballet on Hudson Street. It might seem reasonable to conclude that although keen to develop theory, she saw no need to use it.[12]

This account of how she proceeded contains an element of truth. She *did* pay close attention to everyday street life and observe urban landscapes; she *did* read widely and use analogies to generate ideas; it is true, as noted above, that she rarely read, or defined her views in relation to, social and economic theory in a systematic way. (A neglected exception is the first chapter of *Cities and Wealth*, where she does discuss the idea of influential economists, including Smith, Marx, and Keynes.) And once she had developed, systematized, and written out a set of ideas, she usually preferred to move on, rather than to rehash, revise, apply, or test them. The only (limited) exception is, again, in *Cities and Wealth*, where she slightly reworked, as well as extended, the arguments that she first developed in *The Economy of Cities*.[13] But to call her approach pure induction is misleading. After all, why go to all the trouble of developing a theory or, as she put it in *Death and Life*, "principles," unless you believe that they could usefully be deployed? And how can any theorist jump from fact to finished concept without needing an extended period during which nascent concepts are nurtured, tested, rejected, or refined and put to work? A number of great scholars have written eloquently about this elusive and often protracted process. Joseph Schumpeter, for example, writes of the "endless give and take" of theory and evidence, adding that "though we proceed slowly because of our ideologies"—by which in this context he means theories—"we might not proceed at all without them." Similarly, E. H. Carr speaks of the way in which the historical scholar is "engaged in a continuous process of moulding his facts to his interpretation and his interpretation to his facts. It is impossible to assign primacy to one over the other." This seems to be exactly how Jacobs herself operated, except that, unlike most historians, she was more interested in producing theory than in explicating an event or period. Speaking about "patterns," in the letter quoted by Keeley, she declares, "I am very suspicious of them. I try to find stuff to disprove them." Theory, albeit mostly homegrown, played a continuous role in her thinking.[14]

Of course, some readers may wonder whether Jacobs really did try to probe her own ideas. Her published works lack anything that might reasonably be construed as a test or even a methodical demonstration of facts. For example, it is not obvious that she made any systematic attempt to observe the sidewalk ballet on Hudson Street at different times of day or days of the week, or that she noted how Hudson compared with neighboring streets in the Village. And it is certainly true that she never considered trying to trace the long-term fate of paired samples of specialized, as opposed to diversified, cities. That was not her style. In her letter, she suggests that in each of her books she was trying to produce "a work of art as well as a piece of truth" and that to her way of thinking "art . . . conceals, rather than parades, the laboriousness that went into it."[15] This claim should be taken seriously: Jacobs valued clear prose and a good story, as both a writer and a reader. But it is also an evasion, written by someone who apprenticed as a reporter and who was ill equipped, as well as disinclined, to construct a fully documented narrative. Historians have long prided themselves on their ability to marry good writing with sound methodology, and although historical evidence rarely allows for systematic proof, it usually supports a more thoroughgoing exploration of an argument than Jacobs attempted to provide in any of her books. Undoubtedly, in the privacy of her own study, she probed the logic of her ideas, testing them against her common sense and some readily available evidence, but her notion and methodology of proof were subjective and eccentric.

There is no reason to belabor the point. Charles Tilly wrote, "So long as it expands our range of viable explanations at reasonable cost, I will endorse any morally defensible sociological method." He could have been thinking of Jane Jacobs as a test case, the sort of "unaverage" example that Jacobs herself liked to use. She was terrific at generating ideas, and her polemical style carries great conviction, but proof is another matter entirely.[16]

But where did her ideas come from? It might be argued that the germ emerged not from reading theory but from the sorts of observation, omnivorous reading, and reasoning by analogy about which she liked to speak. This usually seems to have been true, if by *theory* we mean systematic, abstract statements by bona fide theorists. But ideas, theories, and ideologies circulate, mutate, and in piecemeal ways become part of popular discourse. It would be absurd to suppose that, one way or another, Jacobs failed to encounter and in varying degrees absorb big theoretical ideas or that they did not inform her thinking in myriad ways. For example, whether or not she read Schumpeter—and behind Schumpeter, Marx—in the original, she was steeped in ideas about the capacity of capitalism for creative destruction. True, she usually emphasized the creative side, which opened her to the sort of criticism that Lewis Mumford offered of *Death and Life*. Speaking of the forces for urban redevelopment that Jacobs resisted, Mumford observed drily that, although she could not see it, "there is no dividing line between the dynamic forces Mrs. Jacobs favors and the cataclysmic forces she opposes." For present purposes, it does not matter whether Jacobs was wrong or inconsistent on this matter. The relevant point is simply that, from an early date, her thinking was unavoidably influenced by theories not her own.[17]

Just as significant, once she was launched on her career as a writer and urbanist, Jacobs rarely needed to start theorizing from scratch. The preoccupations and ideas of *The Economy of Cities* flowed directly from those developed in *Death and Life*. In *Death and Life*, she concentrated on the social consequences of a fine-grained diversity in land use, but she noted the economic effects, too, notably in her discussion of how Brooklyn had functioned as an "incubator" and "exporter" of small manufacturing enterprises. Here was the seed of an idea that she nurtured and allowed to blossom in *The Economy of Cities*. The subsequent flow of ideas into *Cities and Wealth* was so direct as to seem inevitable. In sum, she steadily grew a body of theory about how and why cities matter. Once launched on this path, certainly by 1960 and arguably earlier, her reading and observations were built upon a core intellectual foundation. Like an owner-builder, she extended this in every direction, but in the end, however idiosyncratically, everything fit together. What she learned from what she saw and read was what she was primed to learn. In 1999, Roger Montgomery told a story about Jacobs's behavior in the late 1960s during a tour that he gave her of St. Louis, which included the now infamous Pruitt-Igoe development: She wasn't interested in anything much except the prospects for Gaslight Square, a downtown restoration project. Montgomery's reading was that, far from looking around in an open-minded fashion, Jacobs had a partial vision, informed by particular concerns, perhaps including where she herself might have felt most at ease.[18]

She was similarly selective of the material she used from the books she chose to read. Two of her own favorite examples will illustrate the point, one from each of *Cities and Wealth* and *The Economy of Cities*. In *Cities and Wealth*, she devotes eight pages to an account of the innovative dynamism of farmers in Shinohata, a Japanese village that, since 1945, has been drawn into Tokyo's urban field. Her argument relies entirely on Ronald Dore's "splendid book" *Shinohata: A Portrait of a Japanese Village* (1978). This is an engagingly written account, of the sort that Jacobs was likely to appreciate, based not only on solid research but also on personal experience. As Dore suggests in the book, and as he has recently confirmed, his understanding is that "one of the things that produced the greatest change in Shinohata" after 1945 was the national government's price support policy for rice. The closest to a theoretical issue that he addresses is the consequences of growing income equality. Apart from a passing reference to price support—an aside within one sentence—Jacobs ignores both issues. Instead, and even though it is treated only briefly by Dore, she makes much of a new method of growing oak mushrooms that was developed by two local farmers because it illustrated an argument she had developed about the roots of innovation. Of course, Jacobs was entitled to pick out this anecdote; to some degree, that is the sort of thing we all do when assembling material in support of an argument. But in so doing, we always need to be alert to the possibility that events are being shaped by a particular historical and geographical context. Significantly, Jacobs did not come to terms with Dore's overall argument, including his account of the national context of local change.[19]

An even better example, and not just because it pertains to my hometown, is her treatment of Birmingham, England, in *The Economy of Cities*. I know Birmingham: I grew up in one of its middle-class suburbs, Sutton Coldfield. During my high school years, I commuted across town to another prosperous suburb, Edgbaston. In between were the delights of central Birmingham, as exotic to my teenage self as Greenwich Village must have been at first sight to Jane Jacobs. There I discovered the pleasures of the Kardomah coffee house ("the KD"), just off the civic square, where my schoolmates and I tried and failed to look cool in our school uniforms; the unfamiliar worlds (Camus's Algiers, Orwell's Wigan) revealed in Hudson's book shop (R.I.P.); the Indian restaurant where, filled with nervous anticipation, I took my first dinner date; and the joys of listening to the Kinks in a booth at a Virgin record store on Corporation Street and hearing Jethro Tull live in Henry's Blueshouse, a sweaty room over The Crown pub. Meanwhile, this textured diversity, as urbanists would now describe it, was being overshadowed by the effects of modernist planning. Every day, I picked my way through the rubble and rebar at a renascent New Street Station, watching the massive Bull Ring redevelopment scheme take shape, as it replaced a large chunk of Birmingham's 19th-century commercial core with a soulless shopping precinct of threatening pedestrian underpasses and car-friendly raceways. Having experienced my own epiphany on the Hudson, when I first read Jacobs's *Death and Life*, at university a couple of years later, I thought I knew exactly what she was describing.[20]

Although she might have, Jacobs did not use the modern Birmingham to illustrate a point. Instead, on a larger and more significant scale than with Shinohata, she used the 19th-century city to illustrate the roots of urban resilience and dynamism. Here she relied heavily on Asa Briggs's *Victorian Cities*. Challenging Lewis Mumford's dismissal of all 19th-century industrial cities as "insensate," Briggs insisted that they varied greatly, the "classic example" of this variation being "that between Manchester and Birmingham." As Jacobs notes, Manchester became specialized with large and efficient factories that polarized classes and stifled innovation, and so it stagnated. Inefficient and impractical, Birmingham fostered small-scale diversity and cooperation between entrepreneurs and skilled workers, and hence technical innovation, thereby thriving into the 20th century. Indeed, although Jacobs does not pursue the story all the way, Birmingham prospered into the early postwar decades, long enough for my father to find work as an accountant at dial-manufacturer James Cook and Sons—precisely the sort of creative small business that Jacobs adored—before it folded, as so many of them did. Jacobs praises Birmingham's early 19th-century lorimers, who made hardware for saddles, because they supplied products to distant as well as local saddle makers, while also learning to fashion other types of goods. Similarly, in the 1950s and 1960s, Cooks' had learned to supply car instrument panels for the local Austin factory, as well as watch dials for local and international manufacturers, justifying my father's only business trip, to Switzerland. So, for me, Jacobs's arguments come close to home in many ways.[21]

And so I can speak feelingly about how, once again, she is selective. To be sure, Briggs himself makes much of the contrasting industrial structure and fates of Manchester and Birmingham. Here, then, more than with *Shinohata*, Jacobs takes her cue from the source material. But still, she ignores much. In the late 19th century, under mayor Joseph Chamberlain, Birmingham became known as "the best-governed city in the world," as *Harper's Monthly Magazine* declared. This status found expression in everything from civic squares and buildings to sanitary schemes, slum clearance, and public libraries. These projects made city life better for everyone, not only lowly lorimers but also silversmiths such as my grandfather, and already comfortable accountants and civic leaders. They attracted international attention and made all Brummies proud. The legacy endured. As she remembered in later years, growing up in a three-bedroom semi on a council housing estate in the interwar years, my mother absorbed and shared this sense of civic pride. In other words, the character and fate of these cities did not depend simply on differences in industrial structure and entrepreneurial initiative. As the noted planning historian Gordon Cherry, himself a Brummie, observes in his historical geography of the city, from the Chamberlain era, "Birmingham was increasingly shaped, governed and provided for by its Council." After all, Corporation Street was named after the city's governing body. Appropriately, more than half of Briggs's chapter on Birmingham in *Victorian Cities* is devoted to the politics and administration of what was known as municipal socialism, but Jacobs ignores it. As with the Japanese rice policy that has shaped modern Shinohata, effective and activist government was not part of the story she wanted to tell or the theory she wished to develop.[22]

Let us be clear: Up to a point, being selective was Jacobs's prerogative.

But let us also be clear and dismiss, once and for all, the absurd notion that she encountered every landscape and every book with a completely open mind. From the beginning, and increasingly through the 1960s and 1970s as she elaborated her system of ideas about cities, Jacobs was continuously juggling her theory with available evidence. What drove her forward was an obsession, a bee that buzzed around her head and whose hum informed all of her best work.

## A MAGNIFICENT OBSESSION

In 2000, Peter Hall distilled the lessons that he had extracted from his magisterial work *Cities in Civilization*. He discussed research suggesting that creative people commonly begin as outsiders, growing up in places removed from the centers of power, but then move in their youth or early adulthood to bigger cities. Recently, Steven Johnson, drawing partly on Jacobs's work, argued that cities have always fostered new ideas.[23] The life and work of Jane Jacobs, a creative thinker fascinated by innovation, illustrate both arguments. Herbert Gans has suggested that when, in her late adolescence, she first visited New York City, this "middle class girl from the working class city" of Scranton, Pennsylvania, was simply "turned on by Manhattan." Indeed, it may be true, as he has also speculated, that Jacobs was especially drawn to Greenwich Village because it reproduced some of the smaller-city ambience of her hometown. Regardless, it is clear that she fell in love, took the interests of the city to heart, and never betrayed them. Her writings for various journals during the 1940s and 1950s, including *Iron Age* and *Architectural Forum*, were early partial expressions of what Roger Montgomery later described as her "city love," with *Death and Life* becoming its first mature statement. The fascination with cities that had been nurtured in New York persisted after her move to Toronto, so that, looking back, Jacobs's biographer Alice Alexiou can plausibly claim that throughout her life, "cities, her passion, moored her."[24]

Arguably, this passion sometimes also unmoored her. Perhaps Jacobs was aware of this. One of her most controversial and implausible claims, made at the beginning of *The Economy of Cities*, is that cities gave birth to agriculture, not vice versa. Based on ingenious speculation, it largely disregarded the available archaeological facts. I myself am no expert on the ancient Near East, but those who are remain unconvinced by Jacobs's claim. Van de Mieroop, for example, states that "Jacobs' theory is based on entirely false premises," while Michael Smith pleads that "if one actually talks about ancient cities, one should look at the evidence." Perhaps Jacobs got the message. In an interview two years before her death, she referred ruefully to her lifelong desire to figure out the roots of urban growth as her "white whale." She was acknowledging that this mission had given her no peace, to the very end. After *Cities and Wealth*, she went on to publish three theoretical books on nonurban topics. In the same interview, however, when asked what book she would most like to see written, she replied: "More stories of ancient cities in the Middle East by archaeologists who are very well trained—and not, you know, sloppy stuff—that would tell us more about the economic relationship [between city and country] in antiquity." She seemed to be open to the possibility that such stories might disprove her controversial hypothesis. What is undeniable is that she took her fascination with cities to the grave.[25]

What made her obsession with cities magnificent was Jacobs's conviction that they matter. It wasn't just that she enjoyed them, was fascinated by their changeable diversity, and wished to defend them. She believed that they are a force to be reckoned with, and not just *a* force but in many ways *the* force. Whether we live in the city or in the country, cities frame and shape our everyday lives; they are leading agents of innovation and change in the cultural as well as the economic spheres; they generate economic growth and, indeed, many of the things that make life worth living. This belief in the significance of cities was simply a given for Jacobs, amounting, as Alexiou has put it, to "an article of faith."[26]

As in other spheres, unquestioned faith has strengths and dangers. In Jacobs's case, a belief in cities sustained her writing and activism in New York City and then in Toronto, where she generally declined to become involved in grassroots activism, concentrating on her writing alone. This belief was the clear focus of her work and her life from the 1940s until at least the 1980s. It is the thread that unites her three major works about cities. Its unwavering, single-minded character surely accounts for much of those books' appeal. But Jacobs's belief in the city as a "protagonist," as David Hill has put it, led her to make some very dubious assertions. Apart from her particular speculation about urban origins, Jacobs often writes as if cities themselves were agents, rather than the settings in which agents, including entrepreneurs, operate. Sometimes this type of shorthand is convenient, but when it hides an unwarranted assumption, it can mislead the incautious reader. The curious thing is that Jacobs pays very little attention to municipal government, which is the one agent that can and often does try to act for the city as a whole. As Tom Bender has noted, Jacobs often "treats cities and their economies as self-regulating entities." By neglecting politics as a sort of side issue, then, she undermines her case for seeing cities as agents.[27]

It was not the city as a political agent that interested Jane Jacobs but its material presence. Indeed, this interest amounted to an obsession. She believed that what really matters are the built forms that embody human activity. This was apparent from the very beginning. In *Death and Life*, Jacobs frames her analysis of the peculiar nature of cities with a sequential treatment of physical elements, notably sidewalks, parks, and neighborhoods. As David Hill perceptively observes, in this work "she is primarily interested with the spatial arrangement of society" within the city, and on this issue she is "single-minded." Although here, as in later books, Jacobs insists on the importance of process, she always views it in relation to the forms that, in her view, shape and enable it. Hence her arguments about the importance of social, and especially land-use, mix. Herbert Gans was perhaps the first to challenge her inclination in this direction, flagging it in the very title of his review of *Death and Life*, "Urban Vitality and the Fallacy of Physical Determinism." But Jacobs's physical determinism, or at the very least determination to tease out the influence of geographical patterns, persisted. In *The Economy of Cities* it found expression, above all, in her argument that healthy cities should contain a mixture of types of economic activity; in *Cities and Wealth* it was embodied in her assumption that distinctions between city and country matter, and in the argument that cities are agents of growth and should become political units in their own right. She saw parallels between processes at every scale, notably through the effects of small-scale diversity. Indeed, in 2004, referring to her perception of the importance of such fractals, she said, "[It was] the only original idea I've ever had in my life." At every scale, then, from the block to the nation and indeed the globe, her thinking was profoundly geographical. She took it for granted that *where* people live and work matters, and dedicated most of her writing life to an exploration of that idea.[28]

## CONCLUSION

Jane Jacobs, I have argued, was a theoretician of human geography at the urban scale. Her interest in cities as physical entities gave shape and coherence to the greater—and I would also say the best—part of her writing. More, her conviction that, understood physically, cities were enormously consequential became the article of faith that sustained her. So powerful was this faith that it hardly needed to be justified; it simply informed everything she did. It was this implicit quality that helped to blind Jacobs herself, and many of her readers, to the theoretical character of her work. From at least the early 1960s, Jacobs steadily built up a systematic body of ideas about cities. Because she saw little need to test or demonstrate these ideas in any formal way; because, once each had been articulated, she preferred to move on, rather than to deploy or defend it; and because the strength of her convictions shunted aside the theoretical insights of other urbanists, she was able to think of and present herself as someone who lived and thought close to the ground. That was only part of the truth, and not the most important part.

To the extent that this intellectual portrait of Jane Jacobs is accurate, it should change the way scholars use her ideas. It requires us to see the main body of her work—at least up to and including *Cities and Wealth*—as an interrelated whole. According to Jacobs, there are parallels and logical connections between vibrant neighborhoods, "impractical cities," and global development. If we are interested in any one of these things, then we need to pay at least some attention to the others. Of course, we may choose not to buy into her arguments at any of these scales, together with the physical determinism that informs them. If so, critiques of her thinking at one scale may offer suggestive lines of argument at others, too. Either way, the implication is that researchers should make more effort to recognize and comprehend the overall shape of Jacobs's work.

Stepping back, the fact that Jane Jacobs is now so widely read should give us pause. By the normal standards of scholarship, in the humanities as well as in the social sciences, her books are deficient in key respects. They assert but fail to demonstrate; they rely on anecdotes; they rarely engage with the ideas of other writers who have tackled the subject. Proudly quirky, they have exerted their influence despite these faults. How so? Their originality is obviously important: As Charles Tilly suggests, we should cut original thinkers a lot of slack. Just as important, she writes well, and with passion. It is regrettable, but undeniable, that a great deal of social-scientific research, including that which falls under the broad rubric of urban studies, is formulaic and bland. There is no buzzing. Historians such as E. H. Carr have the right idea: We need to frame accounts that are persuasive in part because they are lucid and impassioned. Jane Jacobs knew this instinctively, and it is these rhetorical qualities as much as her ideas that account for her continuing influence.[29]

# JANE JACOBS IN DUTCH CITIES AND TOWNS:

## METROPOLITAN ROMANCE IN PROVINCIAL REALITY

### GERT-JAN HOSPERS

"IJburg is 'Jane Jacobs-proof!'" I recently read on the blog of a Dutch planner involved in the development of Amsterdam's neighborhood IJburg. "We have divided IJburg's harbor area in three blocks and three little streets. This will improve the area's diversity, atmosphere and potential for surprise."[1] The enthusiastic blogger is one of the many urban professionals in the Netherlands who are loosely citing Jacobs in order to justify their neighborhood interventions. Jacobs's name has become a warranty of urban quality. Especially after her death in 2006, Jane Jacobs has been rediscovered as a kind of prophet for modern Dutch urban policy. More and more planners across the country are declaring that they are indebted to her.[2] In 2009 the Dutch Jane Jacobs cult reached a climax with a Jane Jacobs festival in the city of Rotterdam that lasted a full three days. Under the title "Ode to an Urban Goddess," lectures, presentations, films, and even urban cycling tours were organized to celebrate the ideas of Jacobs.

In this chapter I explore the ways in which the Dutch deal with Jane Jacobs. When do planners and other urban professionals refer to her? How do they attempt to put her ideas into practice? And to what extent are their efforts really Jacobsian? To address these questions, I start by briefly discussing the reception of Jacobs's writings in the Netherlands over the past decades. Then I review recent examples of neighborhood revitalization in three Dutch cities and towns— Rotterdam, Arnhem, and Enschede—where Jacobs's work has been used as a policy justification. I follow this with a Jacobsian assessment of these policies.

It is important to note that most Dutch policy makers seem to forget the importance of the particular circumstances of time and space: The New York of Jane Jacobs at the end of the 1950s is different from the situation in a

Dutch town today. At the same time, Jacobs was too vague about the policy implications of her ideas. Therefore, her work should not be treated as an ideology but as a source of inspiration.

## JANE JACOBS IN THE NETHERLANDS

Prophets are never recognized in their own countries. This was true for Jane Jacobs after the publication of *The Death and Life of Great American Cities* in 1961. While Jacobs was criticized in the American planning community on account of her plea for more human involvement, small-scale development, and common sense, her work was received reasonably well in Europe.[3] This is not hard to explain: Jacobs defended the historic, mixed city type that can be found everywhere in Europe. After initial reservations, the British liked Jacobs's message, which some even regarded as "a warm but high wind across the Atlantic."[4] The Germans literally welcomed Jacobs. In 1967 she visited Germany at the invitation of planner Rudolf Hillebrecht. In a letter to her family—it was her first trip overseas—she wrote: "In Hannover I actually see the kind of planning, all built, actually executed that I have recommended!"[5] In Scandinavia, Jacobs's ideas also fell on fertile ground. She influenced, for example, the Danish architect Jan Gehl, who advocates a Jacobsian approach to improving urban form. Just like Jacobs, he stresses the importance of human scale in public space and argues for inviting and diverse neighborhoods.[6]

In the Netherlands it took some time before Jacobs's work gained momentum. In the 1960s and 1970s, planners showed little interest in the organic and incremental approach that Jacobs was propagating.[7] At that time, wide-scale demolition and radical renewal were seen as the most appropriate urban development strategies. In interviews, however, Jacobs frequently referred to the Netherlands as a nation where she saw her ideas on vital city life confirmed.[8] Her view of the country must have been colored by the inner city of Amsterdam, which she visited in 1984. Jacobs came to the Netherlands at the invitation of Queen Beatrix to deliver a speech at the Royal Palace, following the publication of her work *Cities and the Wealth of Nations* (1984).[9] Oddly, it was not this book but *Systems of Survival* (1992) that was translated into Dutch.[10] Since the mid-1990s, however, Dutch urban professionals have rediscovered the early Jacobs. Not only cities such as Amsterdam and Utrecht but also old industrial towns such as Heerlen and Hengelo cite her work to ground their neighborhood revitalization policies and reuse of old buildings. The popularity of Jacobs in the Netherlands is clearly reflected by the translation of *Death and Life* into Dutch in 2009.

When the Dutch refer to Jacobs, they mostly highlight the ideas set out in part 2 of *Death and Life*, "The Conditions for City Diversity." Here, Jacobs describes the four generators for diversity in neighborhood districts: primary mixed uses, small blocks, aged buildings, and high density. Since small blocks and high density are quite common in Dutch cities, the policy discourse often focuses on mixed use and aged buildings. Indeed, most quotations of Jane Jacobs in Dutch planning policy documents, speeches, and books deal with the need for diversity in neighborhoods. Thus, mixed use development measures, such as the enabling of residential development above shops and public support for migrant entrepreneurship, are legitimized. Without a doubt, the most quoted Jacobs passage in the Netherlands is this one: "Old ideas can sometimes use new buildings. New ideas must use old buildings."[11] The passage—mostly mistakenly abbreviated to "New ideas need old buildings"—is often used to prevent the demolition of old factory buildings in urban areas.[12] In addition, many Dutch authorities have based their social policies and neighborhood interventions on Jacobs's notions of social capital and "eyes on the street."[13] Finally, the Dutch translation of *Systems of Survival* seems to have paid off: In debates about the roles of the market and the government, Jacobs's distinction between the "Commercial syndrome" (market values) and the "Guardian syndrome" (public values) is regularly employed as an analytical framework.[14]

## DUTCH URBAN POLICY AND THE JACOBSIAN IDEAL

It is not hard to see why Jacobs was enthusiastic about the Dutch capital, Amsterdam, when she visited it in the 1980s. Amsterdam's historic center makes a somewhat messy impression: It has high dwelling densities, a variety of buildings and shops, and a convivial hustle and bustle.[15] Cars thread their way along narrow streets and over bridges, cyclists maneuver their bikes along tram tracks, and most pedestrians cross the lights on red. Along the famous Amsterdam canals we can see stately 17th-century town residences and warehouses now serving as offices for law firms and real estate agencies or as hotels, art galleries, and apartments. In the little streets we pass restaurants and bars, shops selling souvenirs, coffee, and books, and traders of antiques, art, and furniture. When we turn our eyes upward, we can observe that the upper stories of the buildings are often inhabited. The city center is full of people: In addition to office workers, students, and hurrying mothers with their children, elderly people, day-trippers, and foreign tourists also crowd the streets. Life in the historic center of Amsterdam is indeed the vital city life imagined by Jane Jacobs—one of urban quality through diversity.

After Amsterdam, Rotterdam (population 603,000) is the largest city of the Netherlands. Some areas of the harbor city face persistent socioeconomic problems. In 2005 the City of Rotterdam passed the "Act of Rotterdam"— officially named the Act Special Measures Urban Problems—to boost the development of these deprived neighborhoods. Several parts of Rotterdam South—such as the districts Carnisse and Feijenoord—have been designated so-called opportunity zones, a step inspired by Jacobs's work and the French example of *zones franches urbaines*. To facilitate diversity, mixed use, and entrepreneurship in these areas, the zones are subject to different rules than is the rest of the city. Under the Act of Rotterdam, entrepreneurs who invest in their premises and capital equipment receive a subsidy from the city of 50 percent, up to a limit of 100,000 euros. The opportunity zones have induced 38 million euros in investments by more than 500 existing and new entrepreneurs and local real estate owners.[16] A survey revealed that three quarters of these owners would have invested far less if the act had not been in place and 13 percent would not have invested at all. All kinds of businesses have made use of the Act of Rotterdam: shops, bars, health-care providers, service providers, and workshops. The survey suggests that opportunity zones are able to retain entrepreneurs and attract new businesses. Also, the vitality of the neighborhoods seems to have improved.

Another example is Arnhem, a medium-sized town (population 147,000) in East Netherlands that is known for fashion design. Arnhem's Klarendal district has been renovated with the help of insights from Jacobs's work. Klarendal is a working-class area with a mixed population: One-third of the population is born and raised there, one-third is of Turkish origin, and the rest of the residents are students and artists. Over the decades, the vitality of the neighborhood has declined due to closures of local shops such as the bakery, butcher, and florist. Therefore, a group of active residents asked the local housing corporation for help. The corporation, which owns 80 percent of the houses in Klarendal, decided to restructure the neighborhood around the theme of fashion, which fit well with the image of Arnhem as a hot spot for style. Adopting the catchphrase "100 percent fashion," the housing corporation has invested 25 million euros in the setup of a so-called Fashion Quarter in Klarendal.[17] Empty shop premises have been bought and renovated. A former mail distribution center has been transformed into an atelier, showroom, and bar. Moreover, artists and fashion designers can rent shop space for their workshops and dwellings. The new shops offer designer clothes, bags, and hats and attract a lot of window-shoppers. As such, they contribute to a vivid street scene.

The last case example is the Roombeek district of Enschede, a former textiles town with a population of 157,000, at the Dutch-German border. In 2000 the neighborhood was completely destroyed by an explosion at a fireworks factory that killed 21 people. Over the following 10 years, it was rebuilt using interactive planning methods like those Jane Jacobs recommended. In public meetings with former residents and housing experts, four values for the rebuilding of the district were determined: vitality, solidarity, discovery, and familiarity.[18] Subsequently, the original inhabitants of Roombeek could participate in the reconstruction of their destroyed dwellings, while newcomers could build new houses under private commission. To strengthen contacts between the inhabitants of the renovated neighborhood, the city of Enschede invested heavily in ponds, green areas, and walking trails, as well as a lot of neighborhood festivities. The municipality also built a museum and community center in the district and facilitated the location of amenities. Thanks to this innovative restructuring approach, Roombeek has attracted a lot of visitors and media attention. In 2007 the authorities of Enschede even won a Dutch award for their revitalization strategy. The architects Colenbrander and Lengkeek have called the Roombeek district a "neighborhood in plural," a place where "Jane Jacobs is in the air."[19]

## JANE JACOBS—BETWEEN ROMANCE AND REALITY

At first glance, these neighborhood projects are examples of good practices that pay tribute to the work of Jane Jacobs. To be sure, the districts in Rotterdam, Arnhem, and Enschede have been revitalized to a degree: The areas got facelifts, are able to retain and attract entrepreneurs, and certainly enjoy more vivid street scenes now. But on deeper reflection, the neighborhood policies in the three cities and towns can be criticized. This criticism goes further than asking the obvious question of whether the millions of euros that have been invested in these places have actually paid off. Rather, the question is whether the revitalization policies are actually Jacobsian. Was this what Jacobs had in mind when she asked for more human involvement, small-scale development, and common sense in planning and policy? From a Jacobsian perspective, at least three criticisms can be made of these case studies, as well as of similar local restructuring projects in the Netherlands.

First, most revitalization attempts start from the implicit idea that a neighborhood is detached from the rest of its urban context. However, neighborhoods are not islands. Jacobs warned against such an inward-looking approach: "Distinctly separate street neighborhoods are nothing to aim for; they are generally characteristic of failure. . . . Successful street neighborhoods, in short, are not discrete units. They are physical, social and economic continuities."[20] Indeed, experiences with enterprise zones and urban empowerment zones in the United States and the United Kingdom demonstrate that the setup of special economic zones often results in firms transferring their administrative headquarters from adjacent neighborhoods, rather than new development per se.[21] The Dutch call this the "waterbed effect." As can be seen in Rotterdam South, problems are transferred, in the sense that the success of one neighborhood erodes the development chances of other areas. In addition, the Dutch legal system is not suited to the introduction of opportunity zones that are geared to local circumstances. After all, most rules—for example, labor laws and environmental regulations—are determined on a national level. Ironically, if public authorities had not regulated so much in the past decades, there might be no need for the revitalization schemes at all. Many Dutch entrepreneurs, for example, complain about the red tape involved in setting up and running a business. Deregulation would help them more than another subsidy. In Jacobs's viewpoint, governments should always consider why they regulate and how long regulation is actually needed.

Second, local public parties have a tendency to dictate a neighborhood's desired growth path rather than facilitate its organic development. For instance, the local housing corporation in Arnhem chose the catchphrase "100 percent fashion" for the Klarendal district without giving attention to whether it responded to the needs of the inhabitants. This resulted in a mismatch between residents and entrepreneurs. A comment from one of the locals at the opening event for the Fashion Quarter tells us a great deal: "I am more in need of a textiles discounter than these expensive fashion shops. I cannot even pay for one of the bags exhibited in the shop windows."[22] Another danger of a thematic approach to revitalizing a neighborhood is that businesses that do not fit within the theme may stay away. Here, we are at the heart of Jacobs's view: Local authorities should not straitjacket a neighborhood and not strive for homogeneity. Instead, there must be ample room for diversity. Paradoxically, a vital place specializes in diversity—it cannot be captured in one single theme.

Third, it is of great importance to have a sense of reality when it comes to neighborhood restructuring. Jacobs published *Death and Life* in 1961 and based her view on the condition of New York City at the end of the 1950s. However, the reality of the Roombeek district in the provincial town of Enschede can by no means be compared with the hustle and bustle of Jacobs's romanticized Greenwich Village. For example, the number of inhabitants and the degree of diversity in both Enschede and the Roombeek district are too small to provide an economic basis for the variety of amenities that Jacobs experienced in New York. In addition, over the decades, the use of neighborhoods by residents has dramatically changed. In most cities and towns in the Western world, the neighborhood economy has come under pressure. Thus, urban places have lost their distinctiveness.[23] This is due to a combination of factors, including demographic change (the average household size has decreased), technological progress (people are using information technology to work at home and buy on the web), and increased mobility (people are visiting shopping malls at the city's edges instead of making use of corner shops).

## INSPIRATION SOURCE RATHER THAN IDEOLOGY

Among planners and policy makers in the Netherlands, Jane Jacobs has become nothing less than a heroine. In Dutch policy practice, her work is often cited, while she is celebrated as an "urban goddess." It is a paradox, however, that the Jacobsian neighborhood projects set up in Dutch cities and towns such as Rotterdam, Arnhem, and Enschede can be criticized by applying Jacobsian insights. For one thing, policy makers have a tendency to copy and paste good practices from elsewhere. It was perhaps for this reason that Jacobs started *Death and Life* with the following passage: "The scenes that illustrate this book are all about us. For illustration, please look closely at real cities. While you are looking, you might as well also listen, linger and think about what you see."[24]

For another thing, Jacobs was too vague about the policy implications of her ideas. In books, articles, and speeches, she always emphasized the dominant role of local circumstances in the vitality of a neighborhood. For example, in the article "Where to Locate a Bookstore in a City and Where Not to Locate One," she wrote: "All of the elements that make for neighborhood diversity are so interrelated that all elements would be important in some degree for a bookstore's success, but I must admit that I don't know much about bookstores. For all I know, someone right now may be planning a bookstore in a location where none of these elements is present. I hope not; but if so, I wish him luck."[25] When asked about regulatory measures, Jacobs gave vague answers as well: "What is a good regulation? Well, for one thing, knowing why it is in there and when it no longer is necessary. Knowing when a different regulation is necessary."[26] Urban professionals who expect clear answers from Jacobs can only be disappointed. Therefore, they should treat Jacobs's work as an inspiration source rather than an ideology. In a sense, that would be a real tribute to Jacobs—she did not like ideologies at all.

# Time, Scale, and Control:

## How New Urbanism (Mis)Uses Jane Jacobs

Jill L. Grant

As one of the key urban thinkers of the 20th century, Jane Jacobs has had a major impact on the theory and practice of community design, especially in North America. Here, I briefly consider some of the ways that Jacobs has influenced new urbanism—a community design approach that advocates dense, walkable, mixed, and attractive urban settings. Linked to ideas of smart growth and sustainability, new urbanism appears frequently in contemporary approaches to planning new residential areas.[1] Conventional wisdom, as expressed in online encyclopedias such as Wikipedia, traces a direct link from Jacobs to new urbanism: "Although New Urbanism as an organized movement would only arise later, a number of activists and thinkers soon began to criticize the modernist planning techniques being put into practice. Social philosopher and historian Lewis Mumford criticized the 'anti-urban' development of postwar America. *The Death and Life of Great American Cities*, written by Jane Jacobs in the early 1960s, called for planners to reconsider the single-use housing projects, large car-dependent thoroughfares, and segregated commercial centers that had become the 'norm.'"[2]

With its critique of modernist planning, new urbanism reiterates many of Jacobs's principles of good community design, including the importance of diversity, mix, compactness, visibility, and connectedness. In *The Death and Life of Great American Cities*, Jacobs wrote enthusiastically about vibrant ethnic neighborhoods, such as Greenwich Village in New York, in developing the idea that appropriate physical form can create the social and economic conditions that allow urban life to thrive.[3] Her style of architectural criticism favored anecdote over systematic observation; her cryptic quips lambasted the planners and bureaucrats who promoted garden cities, modernist towers, and urban renewal.

To what extent does Jacobs's work explicitly inspire the new urbanists in their theory and practice? Several key thinkers in new urbanism seem to echo her judgments. Some follow her rhetorical strategy of journalistic bombast and bold assertion without specific evidence. Yet new urbanism includes divergent voices and approaches. Its practice and discourse are continually morphing in response to challenges and opportunities, making generalizing about it difficult. Consequently, I will narrow my gaze as I explore some of the links between Jacobs and new urbanism. I focus primarily on the writings of Andrés Duany, as a key new urbanism practitioner, and Emily Talen, as the principal theorist working to integrate Jacobs's insights into new urbanism. I consider how the theories and practices of new urbanism do and do not reveal lingering influences of Jane Jacobs's ideas about physical planning. While Jacobs certainly said many things that the new urbanists find inspiring, key writers conspicuously set aside some of her views about the requirements for good community design and governance. In particular, they overlook some of Jacobs's ideas about the significance of time, scale, and control in generating vital urban environments.

## REQUIREMENTS FOR GOOD DESIGN

While Jacobs often suggested in *Death and Life* that urban vitality emerges from unplanned juxtapositions and time-dependent processes, she also affirmed that good design makes a difference in outcomes. Jacobs argued for creating physical diversity within the urban environment to provide a basis for mixing uses; the mix of uses generates a mix of users and thus produces social diversity.[4] Jacobs identified the multiple diversities that characterized the areas that she loved and postulated causality from the physical to the social. The underlying environmental or spatial determinism of this theory troubles social planners and sociologists such as Herbert Gans, who emphasizes the significance of social networks and individual choices: Gans sees the vitality of ethnic neighborhoods and new suburban communities as deriving from the cultural values and commonality of experiences and class conditions the residents encounter, not from the physical form of the spaces they inhabit.[5] By contrast, the notion that form can shape behavior resonates with physical planners and designers who believe in the efficacy of good design: Jacobs affords them a theoretical foundation to legitimate their work. The prominence Jacobs gave to the influence of the spatial earns her continuing respect within movements such as new urbanism but remains her Achilles's heel for many critics.

Generalizing from conditions in Greenwich Village in the 1950s to the prerequisites for good urban design, as Jacobs did, warrants careful dissection. Jacobs witnessed a particular moment in American culture: the end of one era and transition to another. In the 1950s any responsible adult could reprimand an errant child and assume responsibility for disciplining rowdies on the street. In those days America appreciated its power and sense of cultural superiority; European immigrants celebrated their cultural heritage as they immersed themselves in the melting pot. Jacobs described a period when TV was such a novelty that owners brought sets out onto the street on summer evenings to share with their neighbors. The New York of the 1950s represented a time before air-conditioning drove people inside behind closed windows and before widespread ownership of cars gave working-class people the means to commute to homes in the suburbs. The vitality, social control, and intense interaction of Jacobs's home district of Hudson Street reflected the social, economic, and cultural conditions of that particular era. While conceding that the physical form likely played a role in the urban qualities Jacobs saw in the 1950s, I'm not convinced that form merited the supremacy Jacobs gave it. The short blocks and dense mix of uses of Greenwich Village accommodated the intense street theater that Jacobs described, but it did not produce that interplay. The social and economic conditions of the 1950s, and the complex history of the people and businesses thriving in New York at that time, certainly unfolded within that form; however, as Gans argues, similar working-class dynamics generated lively suburban communities in that era. Social and economic conditions are as much—if not more—a product of time and human history as they are artifacts of spatial configurations.

Throughout their writings, the new urbanists indicate that they covet a similar social moment as that Jacobs described. They seek to build the kind of social vitality that flourished on Hudson Street or that generations of novelists imagined on the front porches of small-town America. Like Jacobs, they conflate urban form with a particular type of cultural behavior. If homes are dense enough, close to the street, on small blocks, and within a mix of uses, people should behave in the way someone—usually the designer or planner— thinks is respectable: conduct fit for upstanding, civic-minded, and responsible citizens. Steps such as keeping windows lit, managing graffiti, ensuring an attractive urban realm, and mixing a small proportion of affordable housing into development projects thus serve as part of a civilizing mission.

Jacobs said relatively little about housing types, but for new urbanism's designs, Duany and his colleagues settled on the small-town American houses of the early 20th century with elevated front steps and porches. The porch is to function as a transition space between the private and public realm and permit occupants to interact with passersby, analogous to the front stoops that Jacobs described a generation earlier. However, in the age of air-conditioning, TV, Internet, and long work commutes, residents may not use the porches in the same ways their grandparents did.

New urbanists define community as the product of particular physical configurations. Space facilitates the functioning of social institutions. For instance, Duany presumes that good design can create conditions that enable sociality, as shown in this comment in *Suburban Nation*: "To begin with the obvious, community cannot form in the absence of communal space, without places for people to get together to talk. Just as it is difficult to imagine the concept of *family* independent of the home, it is near-impossible to imagine *community* independent of the town square or the local pub."[6]

Launching her critique just as modernism and garden city ideas reached their zenith in North America, Jacobs received mixed reviews within the planning community.[7] By the 1970s Jacobs had moved to Canada, where she joined protests about highway extensions and urban renewal projects.[8] Before long, her ideas about density and mixed use were influencing urban planning policy and redevelopment projects in Toronto and Vancouver.[9] Her analysis of the failures of modernist projects in major American cities proved increasingly persuasive as suburban growth proliferated and old urban cores hollowed out. Planners looking for new strategies began to accept the merit of her ideas.

In the early 1980s architect-planners such as Andrés Duany and Peter Calthorpe designed suburban and exurban developments that articulated design principles similar to those Jacobs espoused. The proponents of this new way of building often implemented elements of her prescriptions for physical form without explicitly acknowledging Jacobs's influence.[10] Yet Jerry Adler argued that the new urbanists effectively took Jacobs's prescriptions and codified them for implementation: "Like most visionary architectural schemes, [new urbanism] has sold more books than houses. Many of its principles were enunciated as far back as the 1960s by Lewis Mumford and Jane Jacobs. But their first systematic application came only . . . when Andres Duany and Elizabeth Plater-Zyberk . . . designed Seaside."[11]

Architects Duany and his wife, Plater-Zyberk, initiated neotraditional town planning with Seaside, a small resort town in Florida they designed for developer Robert Davis in 1982.[12] With its compact form, mix of uses and housing types, traditional-style homes with front porches, distinct edge and civic center, and attractive public realm, Seaside captured attention as an alternative to conventional development patterns. Seaside exemplified Duany's commitment to employing the design principles that characterized small-town America.[13] In his writings and lectures, Duany discusses several thinkers who influenced his work, including Camillo Sitte, Raymond Unwin, and Lewis Mumford. Duany's most important intellectual mentor, however, is clearly Léon Krier, the European architect who advocated building according to traditional principles proven in the past.[14] Although his work occasionally includes cryptic quotes and citations from Jacobs, Duany has more commonly drawn on fellow architects for inspiration and supportive arguments. In 1993 Duany, Plater-Zyberk, Peter Calthorpe, and several colleagues formed the Congress for the New Urbanism to coordinate the planning and design principles they were developing, and to initiate a systematic campaign to influence urban planning.[15] Since then, the new urbanism movement has grown into a potent force in North American planning, while scholars such as Emily Talen and Reid Ewing have worked to give it intellectual coherence and methodological rigor.[16]

## WHICH ELEMENTS OF JACOBS'S ARGUMENTS DOES NEW URBANISM ACCEPT?

A close reading of Duany's work finds relatively few explicit connections to Jane Jacobs; however, new urbanists use some of her clever quips to illustrate important points. For instance, the following quote from *Death and Life* appears in several new urbanism books: "The pseudoscience of planning seems almost neurotic in its determination to imitate empiric failure and ignore empiric success."[17]

Despite the paucity of direct citations, many of Jacobs's ideas seem implicit in new urbanist thinking and prescriptions. Like Jacobs, Duany accepts that developing a mix of uses, short blocks, and continuous networks can foster lively streets; that integrating parks, squares, and public buildings with the street fabric enhances the public realm; and that emphasizing the identity of districts helps to connect people to place. Perhaps Duany employs the same style of architectural critique as Jacobs—dispensing with academic citations that might have shown his reading of Jacobs. Or perhaps Jacobs's insights have become conventional wisdom that no longer merit explicit acknowledgment.

Jacobs stipulated four requirements to generate what she called exuberant diversity in the city.[18] Duany and other new urbanists have commonly promoted three of these requirements: Districts must serve multiple functions; most blocks should be short; and medium to high density is required. Jacobs's fourth requirement—that buildings should vary in age and condition at close grain—have received less attention, and this was especially so in the early years of new urbanism.

While Duany focused on designing new urbanism projects and refining tools to implement the vision, academics involved in the movement began to develop its theory. One of the most prolific of these scholars is Emily Talen, a planning professor at Arizona State University. Talen's writings have often discussed the pragmatic and theoretical implications of diversity within new urbanism, trying to make explicit connections between physical form and social outcomes while sidestepping and downplaying the physical determinism that can crop up in the writings of practitioners.[19] In an effort to enhance the academic credibility and authority of the movement, Talen works within new urbanism organizations to encourage practitioners to tone down the overt spatial determinism that the movement's critics find problematic, and to embrace a wider understanding of what diversity can and should mean in practice.[20] She writes, "New Urbanism without social complexity is dreary. In the coming decades this simple truth will compel

New Urbanists to do more than create a physical shell of hoped-for diversity; it will force them to master the art of creating social mix in the same way that they have mastered the art of civic design."[21]

With criticisms of new urbanism mounting within the academy, Talen has sought to establish solid theoretical foundations for new urbanism's principles and practices.[22] In this task, Talen draws extensively and explicitly on Jacobs's work.[23] Talen accepts Jacobs's arguments about the importance of social diversity and the potential that physical diversity has for producing social diversity, saying "there *are* design principles that can help sustain diverse neighborhoods."[24] She has elaborated on "place diversity," which she argues constitutes an element of the conditions required for social and economic mixing.[25] Talen has not abandoned the idea that place plays a role, but she acknowledges its limitations: "I think the aversion to designing for diversity should be addressed by proclaiming what the limitations of design are—having a clearer sense of what can or cannot be accomplished—but not forgoing the idea that physical design has a legitimate role to play in enabling diversity. The appropriate question for planners is not whether the built environment *creates* diversity, but whether diversity thrives better, or can be sustained longer, under certain physical conditions that planners may have some control over."[26]

## WHICH ELEMENTS OF JACOBS'S ARGUMENTS DOES NEW URBANISM SET ASIDE?

While Jacobs suggested that form inherently affects social and economic outcomes in the city, *Death and Life* pointed to other significant factors that new urbanism has tended to set aside in formulating its principles and practices. For instance, in Jacobs's thinking, time, scale, and control affect urban outcomes in significant ways.

Jacobs argued that buildings of varying age and condition provide opportunities for different kinds of uses and classes of people to coexist in a district.[27] "Cities need old buildings so badly it is probably impossible for vigorous streets and districts to grow without them," she wrote.[28] Spaces become meaningful when they are differentiated and organized by temporal processes. Jacobs saw time as a prerequisite for developing social networks and building commitment to place.[29] Social capital and connections emerge as a consequence of the passage of months and years; they cannot be rushed or preplanned. For instance, Jacobs critiqued planners' notion that zoning for corner stores can increase diversity as a patronizing gimmick that failed to understand social and economic conditions.[30]

New urbanism involves building communities over a relatively short period of time with a planned mix of housing types and uses, including corner stores.[31] While some older structures may be retained in redevelopment, most of the structures are built or renovated within a few years. Given designers' concern about the quality of the public realm, little variability in building age or condition results. New urbanists recognize this problem as intrinsic to their practice. "True towns take time; a designer can only provide the ingredients and conditions most likely to lead to a mixed-use future."[32] Differentiated spaces provide a veneer of history but little temporal depth.

Time matters to the new urbanists more as a design reference point than as an unfolding process. Katz notes that the years 1900 to 1920 serve as the architectural and urban model for new urbanism and provide benchmarks for urban design.[33] Critics sometimes accuse Duany of designing old-fashioned towns.[34] Krieger suggests that new urbanism seeks to shortcut the temporal process that transforms the fringe into the center: "Like the ancient Greeks, Duany and Plater-Zyberk prefer to think of the modern suburb as a rudimentary form of habitation, something which precedes the city and thus in need of civilizing."[35] While Jacobs valued the variation in form that time affords cities as they age and transform, Duany argues that compatibility of design and conformity in relation to the street can create appropriate and perhaps even timeless form.[36] For the new urbanists, time constitutes a potential enemy, threatening the longevity of the vision. Hence covenants and design codes limit the potential for design changes, seeking to freeze form in a unique moment in time. The libertarian streak within Jacobs would rebel at new urbanism's unwillingness to let time exact its traditional influence on the city.

Jacobs clearly liked large cities and deplored planners' efforts to create small self-contained neighborhoods.[37] Jacobs thought that planners insisted on working at inappropriate scales, such as the neighborhood unit. She saw meaningful social units at the street level, where neighbors form "webs of public surveillance" that create "trust and social control," and also at the functional district level, or political ward, where significant numbers of residents exert political influence within the city.[38] Jacobs argued that cities have natural advantages over towns and suburbs because size gives them the diversity that generates vitality.[39]

New urbanism works primarily at the neighborhood scale that Jacobs criticized.[40] In its early years, new urbanism was promoted as a better way to design subdivisions.[41] Instead of ugly and dysfunctional suburbs, Duany designed small towns and urban villages with apartments over the shops and civic uses around a town green or square. New urbanism communities are intended to permit a five-minute walk to important destinations and include a mix of living, working, and shopping uses within "true neighborhoods."[42] Within the last decade, new urbanism principles have increasingly been applied to the kind of infill redevelopment projects that Jacobs favored, but greenfield "complete" communities remain part of the practice.[43]

Jacobs reveled in small-scale neighborhoods operating at the street level, such as Hudson Street. She saw these districts as important for organizing political action: Small-scale social networks could mobilize to fight unwanted developments.[44] While Jacobs embraced citizen engagement for urban change, Duany and his colleagues describe such intervention as NIMBYism and decry the tendency of people to resist growth.[45] Jacobs conceived of scale as creating a matrix for social, political, and economic action, while new urbanism accepts scale as a spatial constraint fixed by development economics and planning conditions. In her later work, Jacobs elaborated on her ideas about urban and economic scale, identifying the critical importance of cities in producing wealth and innovation.[46] These later writings get little attention from new urbanist practitioners or writers.

The new urbanists have followed Jacobs's legacy in voicing strong criticisms of conventional planning practice, but their strategies for resolving the problem differ. The libertarian streak running through Jacobs's writings led her to conclude that planning induces conformity, homogeneity, and sterility in the urban environment. She hoped to see cities break with the control that planning imposes, so that social and market forces might operate more freely. Jacobs argued that monopoly planning cannot generate diversity.[47] Building areas all at once cannot create vitality. As Jacobs wrote, "neighborhoods built up all at once change little physically over the years as a rule."[48] Because they cannot update or repair themselves, they are dead from birth.

In drawing on Jacobs's insights, Talen recognizes the inherent problem that new urbanism faces: Comprehensive planning by a master planner is intended to foster diversity.[49] New urbanism applies a unifying vision yet seeks to produce diversity and vitality. Talen argues that planning for place diversity will encourage social and economic mixing, but Jacobs doubted that monopoly control could generate the requisite variety or distributed power.

Duany suggests that because infill alone cannot accommodate the urban growth required, planned developments must continue: New urbanism, he notes, must accept the power that master planning endows and wield it responsibly.[50] In its efforts to promote "authentic urbanism," new urbanism has used the powerful control of the master planner to deploy covenants and codes to safeguard the quality of the public realm.[51] Setting up a home owners association to monitor covenant compliance provides the necessary governance mechanisms to protect the designer's vision.[52] Duany and Talen collaborated to develop a theoretical framework, informed by ecological theory, for explaining and justifying the widespread application of "smart codes" to replace municipal land-use regulations.[53] For the new urbanists, replacing what they see as antiurban planning regulations with urbanistic codes that govern form represents a positive step forward, but both versions reflect the kind of monopolistic control that Jacobs resisted. If Jacobs was correct that places need to have the ability to transform as conditions change, then new urbanism codes and covenants may limit the potential for adaptive responses. Should the traditional forms that new urbanism designers favor go out of fashion in the decades to come, then the districts that feature them may struggle to maintain market relevance.

While new urbanism borrows extensively from Jacobs's concepts in framing its approach to planning and design, it defies Jacobs's teachings in critical ways. New urbanism projects emblematize the monopolistic control of the master planner who designs projects scaled not for appropriate social or political action but because of serendipitous land-assembly factors, and built not to accommodate time but to freeze it in place with codes and covenants. Jacobs's vision of the city as adaptive space within which citizens construct their identities and shape their own prospects in a sometimes messy urban context gets lost in the picture-perfect images of new urbanism.

## Jacobs's Legacy

New urbanism theory and practice reflect Jacobs's vision of lively urbanity: a diverse range of people densely interacting within a finely grained mixed use context. Like Jacobs, the new urbanists reject modernism and garden city ideals, and blame planning for the problems of the North American city. Yet new urbanism does not merely parrot Jacobs's message. Indeed, some of new urbanism's methods violate Jacobs's libertarian notions and reproduce the monopolistic processes that initiated her attacks on planning.

While Jacobs celebrated individual voices and community initiatives in the city, new urbanism has left relatively little space for democratic action or organic transformation of urban form over time. The centralizing power of modernists has been transferred in new urbanism to a new generation of architect-planners and developers who apply their expert judgment through increasingly universalized codes, design guidelines, and preferred forms.

Jacobs understood that her 1961 book transformed planners' theory about the good community, but she expressed reservations about how contemporary practice was implementing her observations and insights. For instance, in 2000 she told James Kunstler that standardized approaches are not helpful: She reminded him that places differ and have to be able to adapt in their own ways.[54] She found the codes imposed on new projects "very constricted."[55] She explained to Bill Steigerwald in 2001 that planners' efforts to create urban centers fail because it is impossible to force urban activity to occur; it happens of its own account where well-traveled routes cross.[56] Jacobs the theorist continued to identify the limits of planning, but the pragmatic practitioners of new urbanism have substituted their own revised form of planning for the earlier version they disdain.

Despite Kunstler's best efforts to entice Jacobs to praise new urbanism, she retained an aura of skepticism. She told him,

> I do not think that we are to be saved by new developments
> done to New Urbanist principles. That's all of the good and I am

very glad that New Urbanists are educating America. I think that when this takes hold and when enough of the old regulations can be gotten out of the way—which is what is holding things up, that there is going to be some great period of infilling. And a lot of that will be make-shift and messy and it won't measure up to New Urbanist ideas of design—but it will measure up to a lot of their other philosophy. And in fact if there isn't a lot of this popular and make-shift infilling, the suburbs will never get corrected. It's only going to happen that way. And I think that it will happen that way.[57]

Jane Jacobs became a guru of contemporary planning even as her admonishments about the undesirability of comprehensive planning fell on deaf ears. She enjoyed the fame that accompanied the television age, when vocal urban critics gained a powerful podium from which to launch their fight against urban renewal. In the 1960s and 1970s, her powerfully written book *Death and Life* became a mainstay of academic curricula being developed for new university programs in urban studies, urban geography, urban sociology, and planning. Her libertarian economic thinking resonated with changing political conditions in the 1980s and 1990s, preserving her relevance in public discourse. Thus Jacobs enjoyed the notoriety of a particular moment in time scaled up by mass media and mass postsecondary education. She was in the right place at the right time, with the right ideas for mass consumption.

To the extent that Jane Jacobs's ideas have permeated North American planning theory and practice, they have come to be linked to new urbanism principles and methods embedded within smart growth strategies and wedded to ideals of sustainability and livability. Certainly it is now challenging to find a plan that does not espouse these ideas and recommend new urbanist principles and methods as the means to achieve them.[58]

The history of planning reveals the systematic simplification of powerful visions in practice. Great theorists run the eternal risk of being only partly understood, selectively quoted, and generally co-opted. Thus, for instance, Ebenezer Howard's garden city committed to urban containment and social reform and Clarence Perry's neighborhood unit designed to protect children on the walk to school now stand accused of complicity in producing suburban sprawl and land-use segregation, even as elements of their visions continue to inspire current generations. New urbanism selectively draws on the contributions of Howard, Perry, and other early urban thinkers and doers, yet Jane Jacobs clearly enjoys pride of place in contemporary discourse. Something of a cultural icon, Jacobs has become an essential ally for new urbanists to (mis)use as they make their claims for public attention and support. As a movement and body of theory that has developed out of practice, new urbanism has found elements in Jacobs's work that resonate, yet practitioners and scholars read and apply her insights selectively. Jacobs's writings continue to provide a touchstone for community designers content to draw upon only the ideas in her work that suit their own approaches and concerns.

# PLANNING THE MODERN ARAB CITY
# THE CASE OF ABU DHABI

RUDAYNA ABDO, AICP, AND
GEOFFREY M. BATZEL, AICP

Jane Jacobs unquestionably transformed Western approaches to urban planning. But in a world made more interconnected by globalization, what relevance—if any—do her classic writings on urbanism have to far-flung places and contexts? Though Abu Dhabi city, in the United Arab Emirates (U.A.E.), today is five decades and 7,000 miles removed from the subject of *The Death and Life of Great American Cities*, it has enjoyed a recent revival in city planning that has seen, consciously or not, the importation of many of the ideals of the physical composition of a successful city first popularized by Jacobs in her seminal 1961 book. How can this be, how deep does the influence go, and does it mean there is a universality to her ideas about livable urbanism?

## THE EMIRATE

Abu Dhabi city is the capital of the emirate of the same name. It is one of seven emirates, or hereditary principalities, composing the U.A.E., a federation of approximately eight million residents, nestled at the tip of the Persian Gulf between the Sultanate of Oman and the Kingdom of Saudi Arabia, and across the Strait of Hormuz from the Islamic Republic of Iran.[1] The U.A.E., formerly the Trucial States, was under British suzerainty from the mid-19th century until the modern nation was founded in 1971.

Whereas the casual observer may be more familiar with the neighboring emirate of Dubai due to the extraordinary real estate boom that occurred there during the 2000s, lower-profile Abu Dhabi is the engine that drives the U.A.E., accounting for about 60 percent of the national economy.[2] Abu Dhabi, which has a population of about 1.6 million—about half a million of whom are residents of Abu Dhabi city—possesses approximately 10 percent of the world's proven oil reserves and is the fourth-largest exporter of crude oil.[3] Unlike other states that have become unraveled by petrodollars, Abu Dhabi and the U.A.E. are long-term success stories—stable, prosperous, and largely insulated from the upheavals afflicting much of the region. While a concentrated program of economic diversification is under way, the hydrocarbon industry is still responsible for more than half of the emirate's economic activity, depending on the price of oil.[4]

Abu Dhabi is on the frontier of global economic growth, wielding an economic influence far in excess of its size. Per-capita gross domestic product in the emirate varies significantly with the price of oil but remains one of the highest in the world at a reported US$90,000 in 2009, which compares favorably with the U.A.E. national average of US$56,000 and the United States average of US$46,500.[5]

Over the past several decades, growth of all kinds—economic, demographic, and physical—has transformed the emirate, reaching a fever pitch from 2005 to 2008, during the huge run-up of oil prices. However, it was not always like this. Until oil production and export began in 1962, Abu Dhabi's economy was traditional, based on the natural pearl industry, fishing, camel herding, and date cultivation. The Bedouin, local nomadic tribespeople, lived much as they had for generations, without paved roads, masonry houses, electricity, running water, or sewerage. Common people lived in *barasti* (palm frond) huts, while the wealthy constructed mud-brick houses. The first permanent roads were not introduced until the 1950s. Then, with the advent of oil and the ascension of Sheikh Zayed bin Sultan Al Nahyan to leadership of the emirate in 1966, a concentrated program of modernization began that continues to this day. The society and economy are under tremendous growth-induced stress, but the emirate has proved impressively resilient, able to provide a high quality of life for its residents while retaining its fundamental cultural integrity.

## THE PEOPLE

The demographic profile of Abu Dhabi and the U.A.E. is unique in that upward of 75 percent of the population is transient: expatriate workers with temporary residency visas tied directly to their employment.[6] Although foreign workers do not have an overt political voice and have only recently been given the right to own property in limited locations, the authorities recognize the need to attract guest workers, so they have set up a system to provide reasonable accommodation to people from all over the world. The foreign workers are economic migrants intent on taking advantage of the Emirati economic miracle for anywhere from a few years to several decades. There is a large contingent of middle- and high-income professionals living in the U.A.E. with their families; they come from around the Arab world, Western countries, and, to a lesser extent, Asia. There is also a large number of people living in the U.A.E. without their families, working for low—sometimes very low—wages in the service sector as domestics, construction workers, and retail and restaurant employees. They come largely from countries such as India, Pakistan, Sri Lanka, and the Philippines. Many of the women in this group are employed as live-in domestics by wealthier families and are not very visible on the streets, while the men are generally engaged in outside work and live either in laborers' accommodations or apartments in the city, so they are more visible in the life of the city.

Expatriates understand, for the most part, that they are guests in a foreign country and accept the terms of temporary residency in the U.A.E. One of these terms is that while they are welcome to become comfortable and active within their expatriate communities, they are not being invited to sink deep roots into Emirati society. Unlike the world promoted by Jane Jacobs, in the U.A.E. political mobilization by the expatriate community—whether at the local level or higher—is simply not part of the package.

The foregoing is not to say that leadership in the U.A.E. is closed or stagnant. On the contrary, Emirati leaders in the modern era have been very progressive toward their own people, focusing not only on ensuring their economic well-being but also on providing a full range of educational opportunities and professional training. A notable outcome is the extent to which women have increased their presence in higher education and in the workforce. Having a skilled cadre of local professionals across all sectors is necessary to offset the enormous presence of, and reliance on, foreign workers and to effectively maintain operational control of the country. While most working Emiratis are employed in the public sector, there is a concerted campaign under way to increase their presence in private companies as well.

Decision making remains strictly the preserve of the locals. Governance is led by the hereditary ruling family, which appoints a council representing prominent and successful extended families. In addition to the modern administrative bureaucracy, there is a historical system of less formal, but no less important, interaction between citizens, centered on the *majlis*. Literally meaning "sitting place," the *majlis* is a forum that occurs in a designated physical location and serves as an important functional part of Emirati life used by the men, including those of influence, for social, religious, administrative, and political purposes. It is the venue at which the heads of households get together, sometimes with their leaders and heads of state, to voice their views and concerns about all matters, personal and political. At the administrative-political level, *majlis* assemblies may be compared to town hall forums, but they take place at regular intervals and are part of the natural rhythm of the community.

Jane Jacobs's premise that citizen mobilization and grassroots activism are core requirements for creating truly citizen-oriented livable communities does not resonate in this context. It is not that her ideas do not seem right—at least to a Western-educated planner—simply that they are too far removed from the current situation to seem relevant. Any strong move in this direction would upset so many deeply entrenched social, cultural, and political traditions that it would likely cause more harm than good. Emirati society enjoys a tremendously rich cultural diversity but has a highly stratified social structure. The government accommodates the whole but only actively involves the few, and it does so through a nondemocratic but grassroots-oriented political system. The overall social and economic stratification has local roots and logical reasons, and it appears to be working quite well in this relatively new and uniquely populated nation.

## THE CITY

Despite its substantial wealth, Abu Dhabi city today is no pearl of the Orient. The skeleton of the city was established in the early 1970s by a young American-educated Japanese planner, Dr. Katsuhiko Takahashi. It has a strong modernist form comprised of a grid of high-speed arterials encasing a collection of rectangular superblocks, which are themselves rigidly programmed with point towers on the periphery that step down to low-density villas in the interior. All in all, it stands as a fine example of the functionalism of the period whose aim was to create a better life through engineering. Whatever one may think today of the beliefs underpinning the design, there was a purity of thought in the original concept of the city that is to be admired.

Over the years, significant intensification has occurred in many of the superblocks, the low-density interiors being replaced by mid-rise development. Urban growth has been driven by the narrow interests of individual property owners and managed by a municipal administration staffed largely by engineers focused on immediate physical planning issues. Relatively little regard has been given to ancillary requirements such as parking, connectivity, or public open space provision, much less a larger strategic vision or concern about the social impacts that different patterns of development may have on the city. The result is a city that is largely utilitarian, only occasionally aesthetic, and integrated or connected along only a single plane, that of the arterial road network. Yet, when one zooms down into the cluttered downtown superblocks, a pattern emerges that shows certain of the virtues of Jacobs's ideal city life, despite the superblocks' inauspicious start: a rich mix of land use; plenty of small ground-floor retail and service uses; middle to high density; cultural, economic, and social diversity; and the vibrant street activity of a 24-hour city. That this rich land-use mix stems from an entirely different source of inspiration than a sense of good urbanism makes it all the more interesting. The factor underpinning this mix is that these properties were gifted by the leadership to individual owners, and because of a great concern for equity in such gifting, each class of property carried similar development rights. Thus, the owners of each property in a group received the right to develop a certain number of total floors on a given floor plate, with the right to ground-floor and mezzanine commercial uses. A wide variety of commercial uses were permissible, with the result being significant diversity of use within a monotony of massing.

In addition to the development in the heart of the city, the rest of the urbanized area grew substantially, and largely contiguously, following the same arterial-superblock configuration. This process has changed in recent years, as the city has outgrown the island on which it was founded and has extended to the nearby mainland. This jump has created a break, both notional and physical, with the past. The idea of a city with suburbs is relatively new in Abu Dhabi, and its implications have both similarities to and differences from what is typically found in North America.

In many North American cities there is a stark and identifiable urban-suburban divide. There are vast dormitory suburbs where people live but do not work. They are built at too low a density to create dynamic street life or efficient infrastructure systems, but they have comfortable residential accommodations and most of the high-quality services that middle-class families seek, such as schools and shops. Then there are the significantly denser urban centers with high white-collar job intensity, where too few people live to provide vibrancy after office hours and there are limited services to attract residents. While this urban structure is in no way accidental, there is now a widespread understanding that the impacts of low density in outlying areas and the divorce of residence from workplace are significant, imposing high social, environmental, and economic bridging costs.

In Abu Dhabi the urban-suburban divide now exists, with some differences. The new suburbs provide comfortable housing and are also of very low density, but they currently lack amenities and services. The city center contains jobs, residences, and services, and is active from sunrise until long after sunset. However, the teeming street life is viewed with ambivalence by the authorities, driven as it is by low-income foreign workers. These people live at very high occupancy rates in tenement apartment towers due to economic necessity and, having no alternative, turn street corners into their living, and sometimes dining, rooms. Many of the middle class still reside in the city center but are not seen in great numbers on the street, favoring their own less-crowded living rooms and the many clubs and hotels catering to the well to do. The local Emiratis are largely absent, seen mostly on the roads commuting and rarely interacting with the street. The rough-and-ready street life of low-income foreign workers has created an image problem for the authorities, who have a vision for their city as a world-class, well-ordered, urban center rather than a crowded Third World metropolis. The solution to this problem has been to begin planning an entirely new, grander, and more sanitized downtown business district immediately adjacent to the existing CBD and retrofitting the existing city center to provide increased leisure amenities and remove many of the overcrowded tenements. Thus, the type of vibrant street life that Jacobs would have found exciting is under threat by a type of City Beautiful movement, although driven less by ideology than by a simple desire for cleanliness and order.

Despite their lack of services, the low-density suburbs have attracted locals and high-income foreigners, creating a version of the middle-class flight that occurred from North American city centers after World War II. Partly this has to do with population pressure and increasing central-city housing prices, but increased affluence, increased growth-induced congestion, and increased availability of suburban options play roles as well. The fix here has been to begin building the services missing from the suburbs and, more important, master plan a major new mixed use city center in the heart of this suburban belt. This new downtown will be based on short blocks, mid- to high densities, a variety of building typologies, and sufficient community uses, retail, parks, and open spaces to accommodate the projected population. In short, the recipe for this new city center contains many of the ingredients identified in Jane Jacobs's work on urban diversity and social dynamics. If the end product even approximates the plan, it will be a very user-friendly and dynamic urban space. It is another quintessential big plan, a top-down vision that this time espouses the creation of a better life through enlightened urbanism—far removed from the incremental process Jacobs had in mind when she wrote *Death and Life*.

## THE PLAN AND THE PLANNING

In 2007, at the height of a vast building boom, a metropolitan growth framework plan was introduced to provide a much-needed strategic vision for a city undergoing rapid growth. Local leadership recognized that they needed new tools to deal with such sustained growth if the overall result was not to be disordered and chaotic. Substantial emphasis was placed on Abu Dhabi city as not only the most important city in the emirate of Abu Dhabi but also the capital city of the U.A.E. The city was to be the showpiece of a nation playing an increasingly prominent role in regional and global affairs. Plan Abu Dhabi 2030: Urban Structure Framework Plan was prepared under the direction of the local leadership by an imported team led by Canadian planner Larry Beasley, formerly director of planning at the City of Vancouver and member of the Canadian National Capital Commission. The plan is founded upon the best modern planning ideals, listing sustainability, livability, connectivity, identity, and cultural and environmental awareness as key drivers. Many of these ideals can be seen as part of the intellectual legacy left us by Jane Jacobs.

And there has been follow-through. As practitioners know, a plan is only as effective as the tools available to implement it, and this plan was followed up by the creation of a brand new strategic planning agency, the Urban Planning Council (UPC), tasked with ensuring that the vision of the plan becomes reality. The UPC, equipped with a substantial operating budget, has grown in three years to a group of more than 200 professionals covering the full spectrum of functions, including policy, urban design, development review, transportation planning, environmental planning, and sustainability.

The creation of Plan Abu Dhabi 2030 as a comprehensive growth framework was a very progressive step for the region, and the plan would stand comfortably beside other similar plans created in North America. What Jacobs would have thought of the new plan is worth questioning. Her views of city life, similar to the logic of her writing, are inductive, rising from the ground up, formed by the interrelationships of individual buildings to the street, nourished by small interactions between the people, which together culminate in a lively and healthy urban environment. Plan Abu Dhabi 2030, by contrast, is a big idea. The plan is deductive, starting with a strong vision of the city as it ought to be and then beginning to work downward through the details. We make this comment more as an observation than a criticism, as the plan was written to work within Abu Dhabi's political and social environment, and a big idea was needed to make a mark.

What is rather more interesting is how Jacobs's ideas have been transformed in the plan into a set of symbols representing good urbanism: diversity, density, mixed use, mixed income. These symbols can then be used in vastly different ways to serve the same larger purpose. The general pattern at work here can be described as the gleaning of small facts from reality, the creation of symbols from the facts, the generating of rules from the symbols, and finally the application of the rules to form a new reality. Whether these new rules are uniformly and reasonably applied will ultimately determine the success of the 2030 plan.

A very strong start brought increased—and, just as important, increasingly standardized—regulation and a harmonized vision to the planning of Abu Dhabi city, and expanded this vision across the entire emirate. But there are recent signs that older ad hoc practices are reasserting themselves, such as projects designated by government leadership as high priority moving forward through the system at great speed, partly or wholly circumventing the newly established procedures. These projects may or may not be government projects and may or may not fit well within the 2030 plan framework; all that really matters is that they have been designated as high priority. While it is too early to determine how these projects will impact the overall success of the new planning procedures, it is quite likely that the new system will work well for the majority of projects but be unable to control certain ones that have high levels of political support. In other words, the situation may not end up all that different from the reality of development in many other jurisdictions.

For an example of the creation of rules from symbolism, we can look at how planners are attempting to resolve an issue they wrestle with in Abu Dhabi: how to frame housing policy in residential suburbs for locals that balances traditional cultural themes with modern expectations. This is an issue very much of the minute, and its resolution will have a significant impact on the ensuing urban form, since tens of thousands of residential units are being planned and built. Urban planners—largely Western, or Western educated—have dutifully researched traditional housing forms in the Arab world and have developed design typologies favoring a dense urban form of traditional courtyard houses focused around narrow pedestrian passageways, as exemplified in old cities of the region such as Aleppo, Syria, and East Jerusalem. These are symbols of traditional city life, the vestiges of which can be found in Bastakia, the oldest section of neighboring Dubai, but not within Abu Dhabi itself. The reality is somewhat more prosaic: a young city comprising freestanding houses placed in the center of large lots, each surrounded by a 6-foot-high privacy wall. A tradition of compound living, large households—averaging 8.5 people, including domestic help—and significant wealth has led to lot sizes of 10,000 to 22,000 square feet and houses that regularly reach 6,000 to 10,000 square feet within urban areas. The scale of these houses, and the need to accommodate cars and modern infrastructure services, make it questionable whether the traditional courtyard house typology can be successfully transposed to modern circumstances. Jacobs would likely have taken issue not only with the scale of the accommodation but also with the element of historical romanticism, or revisionism, in attempting to place a traditional veneer on top of it all.

The UPC, having stepped into a strategic planning vacuum during a period of significant growth, has made the immediate establishment of standards a key element in guaranteeing a minimum level of quality, reflective of the vision established in the strategic plan. Some of these efforts, such as a new form-based development code and a pedestrian-focused street design manual, reflect the livable-city planning legacy of Jane Jacobs. Others, including a one-size-fits-all community facilities framework and a series of extremely prescriptive master planning efforts covering much of the metropolitan area, reflect a lack of trust by the planning agency that the development community will deliver high-quality livable urban spaces if allowed too much flexibility. While ensuring minimum standards, this approach will likely not allow for the wide variety and uniqueness of a city built out organically over time.

## PUBLIC PARTICIPATION

Jacobs's approach to public participation and grassroots mobilization has no parallel in the case of Abu Dhabi. The political system and circumstances are just too different for her ideas to be particularly relevant. For Jacobs, the city belongs to citizens, whereas in Abu Dhabi true citizens are in a sharp minority and are dealt with using a quite effective approach that mixes tradition and modernism. The rest of the population is impermanent—legally, physically, and psychologically. Noncitizen residents have limited property rights, exist on temporary visas, and fall into socioeconomic and ethno-linguistic groupings more reflective of a cosmopolitan developing city than a postindustrial city of the West. Jacobs's beloved Toronto comes fairly close to Abu Dhabi in terms of diversity. But in Toronto, noncitizens—even the newest arrivals—have a level of commitment to place that is unseen in Abu Dhabi. This shows that citizenship, or the promise thereof, does affect commitment to place. If a city can be caricatured as a single vast mixed use development, then Abu Dhabi is a long-stay hotel resort with accommodation varying from one star to seven, with a limited number of luxury penthouse condominiums perched on top for the permanent residents.

The UPC is trying hard to create and apply good planning principles and has undertaken a limited number of Western-style workshops to discuss local planning issues. Though this participatory planning is generally considered successful, the jury is still out—and experiences are too limited—to determine whether it will prove to be more effective at conveying the opinions and wishes of the community than the locally practiced *majlis* forum. As for more active or overt forms of dissent, petition signing and protests simply do not form part of the local culture and would not be undertaken by the expatriates worried about having their visas revoked.

## JACOBS'S MAIN THEMES

Four of Jacobs's key tenets of ideal urbanism—diversity, mixed use, high density, and an active public realm—play out a beautiful performance for analysis and critique in Abu Dhabi. By the nature of the composition of its population, diversity in Abu Dhabi is rich at most levels and has been since the country urbanized. As with so many other aspects of life in Abu Dhabi, diversity is experienced differently by the three discrete segments of the population: the local Emiratis, the foreign professional workers, and the foreign blue-collar and service sector workers. The minority in the streets and denser urban neighborhoods of Abu Dhabi are the local Emiratis, who are far overshadowed by the foreign working-class majority. Emiratis have moved away in large numbers from the central city to the mainland. When seen publicly, they are most often working in government offices or relaxing in shopping malls and hotels. The foreign professionals tend to work in the private sector and gravitate toward the same shopping malls and hotels, but they have limited direct interaction with the locals. For about eight months of the year, when the weather is very pleasant, the foreign blue-collar and service sector workers linger freely in arguably some of the safest streets—in terms of personal security but certainly not road safety—in the world today. The city is trying hard to create new places and events to encourage public congregation, such as a public beach along the prime waterfront stretch and festivals where people of all ages, incomes, and tastes come together to enjoy local and imported culture. It is situations like these in which the voice of Jacobs can be heard resonating: Mix the races, incomes, and tastes and have them rub shoulders in their (temporary) home city. For urban planners in the emirate, the challenge is addressing the needs of each of these groups while remaining focused on the prime directive: the creation of a modern Arabic capital city reflective of the culture and tradition of the Emirati people.

As far as the mixed use composition and density of the city goes, by many counts central Abu Dhabi has got it right. The city is thoroughly intermixed, including the vertical mixing of uses, and land is used at significant but not choking density. The result is that intense residential and commercial uses occupy just about every block in downtown. Land regulations in most downtown blocks allow for full ground-floor and mezzanine commercial activity, with either residential or office uses above. With relatively small plot sizes and an inner grid of smaller streets within the superblocks, buildings are typically designed with no backs or secondary façades. Rather, they tend to have multiple entry lobbies and individual accesses to the small retail outlets that wrap the buildings. The result of this mixed use intensity is a bustling city that is active from early in the morning to late in the evening. The symphony of daily events in Abu Dhabi city would, no doubt, tickle Jacobs's fancy. However, it is this bustling street activity that some people desire to clean out of the existing urban form, especially as it is mostly performed by the "wrong" segment of society—the working class. If such gentrification were to take place, Jacobs certainly would not think highly of the transformation.

There is also little doubt about what Jacobs would think of the newly planned and developing suburban communities on mainland Abu Dhabi. These areas are being developed in response to pressure from local Emiratis for large single-family housing lots. The resulting densities—three to six units per acre—are very low, and there are correspondingly low levels of supportive commercial uses, which will no doubt struggle to create the pedestrian activity present in the central city. While such low densities go against the desires of the professional planners, the provision of housing is an important part of the social contract between the emirate's leaders and its people, and the fundamentals of this social contract are not up for discussion. These developments are prime examples of the high-priority projects mentioned above that are challenging the newly established planning systems.

## CONCLUSION

In terms of Jane Jacobs's intellectual legacy, there is something paradoxical occurring in Abu Dhabi. On one level many of her views relating to the physical structure of cities have been adopted since they were embedded in Plan Abu Dhabi 2030, including a belief that city form should enhance connectivity, promote a vibrant street life, provide parks and public spaces, and allow for mixing of different groups in the public commons. Jacobs would certainly not have believed that these principles should be mandated from above, but in our opinion the top-down form is necessary in order for them to be successful locally, as all governance in the emirate is clearly structured from the top down. There has also been the kind of follow-through on the plan that would be the envy of any North American planner: the creation of a new planning agency that is wholly focused on the plan's refinement and implementation, and that has been given teeth and funding to execute this mandate. While it would be tempting to dismiss this step as government lip service to better urbanism, there is absolutely no doubt that the outward appearance of the city as it develops from here onward will be more uniformly hospitable to the person on the street in a way that would likely not displease Jacobs.

However, while this positive change is occurring at the street level, underneath there is a structural change taking place that is moving the city in a starkly different direction. The move to sanitize the urban street life and the development of large dormitory suburbs inhabited by the mobile local and foreign elites clearly would not sit well with Jacobs. Cleaning up the town risks greatly reducing the vibrancy of the urban street life and poses real questions about what the working-class foreigners are to do and where they are to do it. The development of the suburbs will, over time, create many of the same problems that are proving to be so difficult to overcome in North America. And while the planners in Abu Dhabi are cognizant of the risks inherent in both these changes, neither is fundamentally negotiable. As elsewhere, there is no clear path forward in Abu Dhabi on planning for the urban poor, and there is no sound economic or social cure for the dormitory suburb.

In sum, the literal relevance of Jane Jacobs's seminal works on urbanism to the evolution of planning in Abu Dhabi is not significant. The social and cultural chasms between the cities she wrote about and Abu Dhabi city today are just too vast. Ultimately, decision making in Abu Dhabi is autocratic. While current thinking supports planning philosophies rooted in Jacobs's ideals, at the end of the day the local Emirati minority's wishes will dictate the development of the city, and certain fundamentals of Jacobs's principles are simply not supported by, or relevant to, the local culture.

# Jane Jacobs, Andy Warhol, and the Kind of Problem a Community Is

## Timothy Mennel

Andy Warhol and Jane Jacobs both came to New York City from industrial cities in Pennsylvania—Jacobs from Scranton, Warhol from Pittsburgh. Yet the kinds of people and social values that they found and cultivated in New York could not have been more different. Their divergent perspectives point to notions of community that continue to resonate today—and that continue to be in conflict with each other. Warhol's concepts of urban life, such as they were, undercut some of the ideals that Jacobs's work popularized and offer a hint as to why those ideals have not found—and perhaps cannot find—greater traction in the contemporary city.

Throughout 1961—the year that Random House published Jacobs's *The Death and Life of Great American Cities*—Warhol had experimented with new styles of painting, a medium that was largely new to him. Most of his work prior to this time had been drawings, particularly for advertising campaigns and fashion magazines. In December of that year, he began the series of paintings that was to redefine his career as an artist and also point to a different, cooler conception of urban life: the Campbell's soup-can paintings.[1] In the same period, he created seven paintings known as the *Dance Diagrams*, which are large-scale reproductions of the images found in guidebooks that show people how to execute particular dance moves—which foot to move when, and where to put it.

Warhol's paintings stood in sharp contrast to the "hot" Abstract Expressionism that had dominated the New York art world in the 1950s. Overtly macho artists such as Jackson Pollock had created a style fueled by emotion, personality, and energy that had come to embody a postwar American sensibility: robust, idiosyncratic, and ultimately exclusionary. Representational art had not fallen out of style so much as been hurled out of it. Yet beginning particularly with the soup-can paintings, Warhol created works that did not seem to admit emotion or even point of view; nor did they evince much of a personality. They seemed to hide in plain sight. Moreover, they were flatly representational, depicting icons of lived American culture—cans, labels, Green Stamps, car crashes, movie stars, flowers, and so on—without appearing to have anything to say about them. Was the picture of a soup can a deadpan critique of American consumerism? Or was it a statement that American identity was better reckoned with through its physical realities than through the emotional states of particular artists such as Pollock? The last person to ask was Warhol, who cultivated a distinctly cool affect. Nothing really meant anything, he would tell people; he just liked soup and ate it every day for lunch. Whether he meant this affected disinterest and whether he actually saw himself as a kind of machine are questions that have occupied countless art historians.

Warhol's early works were hand-painted, not silk-screened as many of the famous later ones were, but he took pains to disguise the material labor involved in their creation. To make the *Dance Diagram* paintings, Warhol used an opaque projector to cast images of dance steps from two popularly available books—*Lindy Made Easy* and *Charleston Made Easy*—onto canvas, where he traced and then painted them. When they were exhibited, the paintings were installed on the floor, as if viewers might step onto them and use them, rather than regard them as aesthetic objects.

Though the Campbell's soup-can paintings are better known, the contemporaneous *Dance Diagrams* resonate more with the notions of urban community that Jane Jacobs was putting forth in *Death and Life*—not least because they draw attention to the mechanisms of control that underlie social engagement, even in situations as casual and seemingly spontaneous as Jacobs's "ballet of the sidewalks." Unlike Warhol's paintings of objects from daily life (such as the soup-can paintings) or of icons of contemporary society (such as the slightly later portraits of Liz Taylor, Marilyn Monroe, and Elvis Presley), the *Dance Diagrams* show a socially conditioned process by which two people engage with each other—a *ritual* of participation, in other words.[2] Much as Jacobs sought to look at the streets of the city with fresh eyes and to draw attention to their nuances and functions, Warhol seems to be asking viewers of his paintings to consider the codes and gestures by which people move through social space. While social rituals such as dance steps do provide a mechanism by which people can reach outside of themselves and join a community (in this case, of other dancers), they also point to the essentially constructed nature of that community: There is nothing intrinsic about a community of dancers save that they have all consented to observe the codes required to be such a community.

The deeper question here is what participating in a dance actually entails. Is there a categorical distinction between following a diagram of dance steps and dancing per se? Those who do not need a diagram are likely better and more fluid dancers, but knowing the codes and expectations is a critical part of participating successfully in the "ballet." Here, though, lies an inherent judgment: At some point individual behavior will cross a line beyond which a person can be said to be "not dancing" or not functioning as part of a certain kind of community. That judgment itself is the product of social expectations and codes—and it is here that we can see the most critical divergence between Warhol's conceptions of urban life and community and Jacobs's. Where Warhol is in effect asking why society has created particular forms for physical and social interaction when there are so many other possibilities, Jacobs seems not to have seriously questioned the validity or socially constructed nature of the ballet of the sidewalks that she depicted. Rather, she posits it as an ideal, and perhaps even a norm.

While Jacobs became well known for putting forth a model of urban community that was at odds with the dominant mentality as expressed through the various postwar urban-renewal programs, the contestation over the nature of urban community was a conversation that had more than two sides.[3] Different conceptions of the city abounded both in policy circles and in the popular media, with greater nuance than retrospective views have often allowed. Some of the depictions of the city that resulted then fueled the idea that the city was intrinsically dangerous—an idea that Jacobs worked hard to oppose—but others pointed out that the city was, for better or worse, not a small town.[4]

As has been noted often, Jacobs's work is characterized by belief in a certain kind of community—one with clearly defined roles, a mix of classes, and a constancy of activity in the streets and of people watching that activity. This kind of "warm" community is depicted as lively and engaged, with positive social benefits arising from the free association of people who have different functions and beliefs but who all exist within a circumscribed social environment called the neighborhood.

Jacobs contrasted this kind of environment with those being created in the modern city, places defined by coldness in building materials and, by extension, in social qualities. The communities that were being formed in these new buildings and re-formed neighborhoods were not, by her lights, real communities, in that they were not only transparently artificial but also reductive, turning people with local jobs and functions and connections into residents who worked elsewhere. For Jacobs, what people did for a living was intrinsic to defining who they were and what their neighborhoods were like.

It does not diminish the value of the kind of social environment Jacobs favored to point out first that it posits a healthy neighborhood as a kind of panopticon, with a decided lack of privacy and anonymity. More important, however, is that this conception of neighborhood seems to write out significant portions of actual urban experience.[5] Where, in these idealized neighborhoods, do sad and angry men hover in bars and get into fights? Where are the lonely, the unhappy, and the unwell? And where are those who reject social conformity, who choose to be defined not by their jobs but by something else, such as personality or infirmity? Where are all the people on the margins—criminals, artists, or a combination thereof? Where are the dropouts, the beatniks, the inept, the clueless, and the lost? Jane Jacobs dreamed a society, but it was a society of a certain kind of conservative cast, based on function and ultimately order. It was a society of productive, social, mutually supporting individuals. It was a society comprised in large measure of well-adjusted libertarians who all had places in the dominant economic framework and who would unite to pursue common self-interest—specifically, the preservation and continuation of their shared social environment, their neighborhood. It was a society without an internal life beyond Jacobs's own delight in it.

As his career and personality took new shape in 1961 and beyond, Warhol generated a kind of social environment that is at odds with Jacobs's conception of a community and also not much in tune with what contemporary planners look to when trying to create vibrant, engaged public realms. That notion of community, however, can be seen as a more realistic assessment of what community—that is, dealing with other people in all their complexity and potential unruliness—entails. As Richard Sennett has noted, many traditional ideals of community are rooted in the *fear* of participation, even as they claim otherwise.[6]

Warhol's crowd was a self-consciously aloof set of artists, photographers, musicians, actors, show-offs, talentless cretins, fools, and geniuses. Few of them held traditional jobs; many of them lusted for fame. They formed a world that was profoundly influential on the American conception of the city—in that it both celebrated impersonality and disengagement and created the basis for today's literally spectacular cities, where significant economies are based on the touristic gaze (what there is to see) and the culture of celebrity (whom you might see there). Countless people come to New York every year in the hopes of seeing something more spectacular or someone more famous than what and whom they can see at home. Andy Warhol helped create this kind of city: a city based on no one caring who the hell you are, until you become a star. While Warhol was famously nonjudgmental, blandly pronouncing whatever people were up to as "great," he nonetheless sought to provoke—which in the early 1960s could mean creating flat, detached paintings of soup cans and dance steps that befuddled prevailing norms. Like-minded spirits might find one another in Warhol's city, but overall it was a cold place—one where you had to make your own meanings, find your own friends, and create your own style. And even if you could do that—and there was no reason to think you could—you might still get shot by someone who couldn't handle the cattiness, the rejection, and the lack of social support that typified the lives of those who hadn't yet found the way in.[7]

Warhol's world may be no model for what planners today consider a vibrant and lasting and productive community, but it has been a significant influence on New York's visual and financial economies, and understanding it is important to understanding the nature of urban community today. New York's national influence being what it is, the power of this economic conception spreads beyond urban community, even, to the more general question of what we mean by *community* at all in America today.

Lots of strivers and misfits, self-styled and otherwise, arrive in the big city every year, and they are not all searching for what Jane Jacobs wanted to find or create there. Some of them are looking, for any number of reasons, to get out of the small towns they come from, not to import those places' values into their new environment. Much as Jacobs loved the vibrancy and energy that arise when people of various classes and purposes come into contact with one another, she sought to celebrate and cultivate what amount to small-town values in the big city. But Andy Warhol went to New York to get out of the social backwater of Pittsburgh and to re-create himself by his own lights and by the lights of fame. Andy Warhol became a modern urban creature—a mirror and a product of the speculative capitalism that fuels the worlds of art and finance that have thrived in New York as nowhere else in America—in a way that Jane Jacobs never did.

Warhol and Jacobs were different species of libertarians. In the early years of his famous Factory environment, Warhol created a space where people could—thanks to the combination of his largesse and professed disinterest in actual personalities—do whatever they wanted, whether brilliant, useful, or stupid. He disclaimed responsibility for what people did in his orbit, and in significant ways he also forswore control over them. This environment provided the kind of community, the kind of support, and the kind of social and intellectual ferment he desired.[8] The archetypal version of the Factory was in midtown Manhattan, surrounded largely by offices—meaning that Warhol's ideal community at this time was not humanistic (being, after all, a factory), not street oriented, and not really in a residential neighborhood. Indeed, the Factory was Warhol's workplace—he lived with his mother on the Upper East Side. But the community that gathered there, and the art, films, and music that emanated from it, had a profoundly transformative influence on the culture of New York and far beyond. It is not difficult to see Warhol's influence in art but also in punk music and rock and roll, in celebrity journalism and affectless fiction, on the spread of irony as a cultural weapon and pose, in the rise of loft living as both a way of life and an aesthetic, in the blurring of boundaries between public and private personas, in the art world's casual and frank commodity fetishism, and in the cultural dominance of hipsters and kidults. Some of these developments may be phenomena to be lamented, but their cultural weight cannot be discounted. More important, the idea that a city is a place where young people go to cultivate identities gained significant force from the example of Warhol's Factory.

Jacobs, in her contrasting brand of libertarianism, sought to free individuals not from cultural constraints or norms but from what she saw as the blind or arbitrary dictates of government. She believed that people, on their own and free from what she saw as the nonsense of bureaucracies, would work toward productive and beneficial social ends, simply by living their lives, albeit within the dominant economic and social system. Warhol cared about that system only to the extent that his material success within it enabled him—and by extension those around him—to live as they chose. Warhol himself was apparently not as wild a creature as some of those around him were, but it is safe to say that he valued people who used their freedom to push society's boundaries more than he sought out those who contributed to a Jacobsian web of mixed uses and, perhaps worst of all, served as invasive "eyes on the street."

Jacobs praised those who came together to stop highways, build housing, or develop economic capacity. She even wrote admiringly of those who came together under the banner of nationalism. But it seems unlikely that she would have had much praise for those who came together in refuge from the dominant culture or in pursuit of fame for its own sake, or who were united by their very disdain for the *gemütlichkeit* values that Jacobs found in the Greenwich Village of her era. Jacobs failed to see the value of impersonality in the city, whereas Warhol (perhaps partially on account of his homosexuality, which he often masked as asexuality) engaged with that impersonality—both in the concrete of the city and through his impenetrable social mask—to help create a kind of urbanism that itself engages with and reflects the complex and large-scale economy and society we actually live in.

Interestingly, one of the few political stances that Warhol took in the 1960s was against Robert Moses, whom many have styled as Jacobs's ideological opposite. But Warhol had no statement to make against Moses's work on urban renewal, highways, or housing projects, as Jacobs and her allies did; rather, he was protesting the censorship of his work by Moses (with help from Nelson Rockefeller and others) at the time of the opening of the 1964–1965 World's Fair in Queens.[9] Warhol's engagement with Moses was over art, not politics or land use or community values. Most tellingly, Warhol did not particularly publicize the bout and largely backed down from Moses.

The greater irony here is that Jacobs made her greatest impact on planning by weaning planners off the idea that they held some special key to understanding humans, their behavior, and their environments. And yet it is easy to feel as if she ultimately exchanged one ideal for another, neglecting social and economic complexity in favor of a sentimental picture of urban community.

But if Jane Jacobs is the patron saint of anything in the urban environment, it is conflict and change. It is a misconception to see in her work a desire for steady-state solutions—particularly as she went on from *Death and Life* to explore the dynamic relations of urban development and economic growth. It is perhaps here that her analysis has been turned most to caricature, by allies and enemies alike. Jacobs certainly opened the door to the interpretation of her work that has predominated among new urbanism and other derivative movements, but the real flaw is not that she envisions a big-city neighborhood as a small town so much as that her libertarianism supports the fantasy that urban dwellers would self-interestedly choose such a world over any other. Her belief in small-town values is traditional and understandable, given her background; but her hope for a natural instinct toward cooperation and socially sustaining behavior verges on the starry-eyed. This might in part explain why attempts to build communities based implicitly or explicitly on this template often fall short of the ideal.

The creation of a genuine and effective community—if we posit the possibility of such a thing—requires not only work and sacrifice but, in critical dimensions, a shared sense of purpose. But in truly complex cities shaped by a multitude of agendas and populated by genuinely diverse populations, such shared purposes tend to arise only among communities of like-minded individuals—or, on a larger scale, those motivated by nationalist fervor, something Jacobs expressed a qualified admiration for in *Dark Age Ahead*. Mobilizing people with shared stakes and beliefs is one problem, but urban complexity inherently diminishes the homogeneity that propagates such solidarity.

Andy Warhol's Factory was an unstable and upsetting environment. Excesses of all sorts took place within it, and for every white-hot innovation there were hours of tedium and artworks that seem cheap or underbaked. But at its heart, the messy vitality of that kind of urbanism demonstrates how a mass of individuals can come together—all the while fighting and pursuing their own agendas—and generate a transformative kind of community. The implication of this is that a "cold" community—based on self-interest and disengaged from the issues and mentalities and prejudices that tend to inform "warm" communities like Jacobs's ideal—can have more impact and more resonance in the contemporary city because it recognizes and incorporates the essential driving selfishness of urban individuality.

Accommodating antisocial or even irrational qualities remains a significant challenge in planning practice today. Doing so in a manner that is not condescending or merely lip service is an even greater one. Recognizing that what we mean by "urban community" needs to accommodate those who find value in impersonality and those who thrive in modernist landscapes and those who do not wish to have any eyes on their street is a critical aspect to developing urban planning practices that have value and even support across society. When planners neglect to do this and instead promote a narrow spectrum of essentially middle-class and nonurban values, it is small wonder that the environment they hope to shape does not respond. The nature of the city is that it is heterodox and in many senses beyond the control of any ideology, no matter how well intentioned.

Political resistance to the imposition of ideology is perhaps more visible today than it has been in other times. More than disputes over ideology or policy alone, there is a serious contest under way over the nature of the state and its power. For some, the need to be self-determinative outweighs the need to contribute to or take responsibility for a larger society.

A related belief in the essential virtue of untutored wisdom can be found in Jacobs's work, and it is possible to draw a line from the kind of community empowerment that Jacobs promoted in *Death and Life* to the present overvaluing of individual perception that is evident in many public discussions of community planning. In 1961, it was unquestionably the case that individual members of communities were not listened to enough by urban planners and the other professionals across the political spectrum who brought urban renewal programs to life; today, it is too often the case that planners and others do not insist on the value of their education, training, and analytical abilities. The overprivileging of the individual perspective is part of a larger shift in the American mentality, of course, and is not constrained to urban planning issues.

Certainly, contemporary rhetoric ostensibly arguing for less government control over daily life arises from a variety of sources, though it rarely leads to actual reductions in government size and investment. Yet this rhetoric and Jacobs's work exist on a continuum, at one end of which is today's violently proud know-nothingism. There are distinct echoes of Jacobs's libertarianism in both American antigovernment rhetoric and, even more vividly, in the movement under way at this writing in Britain toward a "Big Society" under the prime ministership of David Cameron. In this scheme, the central government is ending or scaling back many of its traditional activities in the belief or hope that individuals or small groups will pick up the slack. While the ideas undergirding the Big Society have a complex pedigree, it seems clear that any political program requiring the governed to actively embrace responsibilities that were previously handled by the government will meet with much more success if the people in question see themselves as a "community" that is pushing away the paternalistic hand of government and caring for itself, rather than as people being denied basic privileges of life in a democratic society. In a strange convergence, the British appear to be betting—much as Jane Jacobs did—that promoting the notion of community might produce community itself. There is something perverse in the spectacle of community empowerment being used to eliminate or cripple programs that in past generations have been seen as critical to the shared pursuits of well-being that have often defined the purposes of democratic governance.

This is, of course, not to say that Jane Jacobs sought to promote an ideal that would in the long run diminish communities' strength. But the implications of her thought—and the uses to which it has been and is put—lead us to situations that require full engagement with the complexity of urban experience. The cities we have today are in many ways more Warhol's than Jacobs's—and that's not entirely to the bad. Warhol did not promote the idea of community, yet he helped create the actual thing, even if it isn't of the kind that Jacobs or most contemporary planners might endorse. Whether or not the results are aesthetically or politically pleasing, our cities nevertheless must make room for the misfits, the self-defined, the antisocial, the anticommunitarian, and the spectacular as much as they do for tight-knit communities and engaged citizens. But the dance among these interests and forces is a difficult one, and there is no simple guide to how to perform its steps.[10]

# A Chinese Perspective

NATHAN CHERRY, AICP

America's post–World War II economy has been an engine that fueled sustained investment in cities, yet this period has seen relatively modest growth compared to what China's urban areas are experiencing now. For example, the population of New York City's major metropolitan area in 1940 was about 8 million; 70 years later, it is about 19 million—a 240 percent increase. By comparison, Shanghai, which had about 4 million people in 1940, is also now home to around 19 million—a growth rate of 475 percent. The cities that were part of Deng Xiaoping's special-economic-zone initiatives have grown even faster: The population of Shenzhen, a village of fewer than 100,000 in 1980, has grown to more than 10 million—a nearly 10,000 percent increase.

If we are going to begin to understand the impact of Jane Jacobs in China, we first have to put this amount of development in its appropriate context. In fact, the growth of Chinese cities over the past generation is analogous to Western urban expansions of the 19th century, not the 20th. Now, as then, the motivation for massive immigration into cities is proximity to jobs. Cities such as London, Paris, and New York grew at similar rates in the 19th century because of core competencies in manufacturing, banking, and movement of goods. In each of these cities, "big idea" planning drove public investment decisions, which helped to ensure long-term livability in the modern era. The decision makers were not that large or diverse a group, but from them came some of the important planning interventions that make these cities great today. New York's Central Park, London's Underground, and the grand boulevards of Paris all transformed their cities, and all were informed by a desire to create change for the good of the community in the long term.

By the 1950s, the economy and demographics of New York City were relatively stable, and the supporting infrastructure was already well established. The subway could take you wherever you wanted to go, regardless of your economic stratum; Central Park was the ultimate urban amenity; and jobs existed in many sectors: manufacturing, consulting, entertainment, health care, and education. Affordable housing was provided through rent control. Robert Moses and others had built many important public works and numerous parks and playgrounds that improved living conditions across the city. The fact that Jane Jacobs was so generally critical of the field of planning in *The Death and Life of Great American Cities* shows how good the quality of life was in New York by that time. Isn't it a testament to planning having already done much of its essential job that, as Jacobs claimed, its more recent work began to threaten earlier successes? If we can accept that she could have slightly misread the positive impact of planning on her own era, does that change how we assess her impact on the field today? And, going further, how can we translate that impact in North America to understand the practice of planning in contemporary China?

## Understanding the Economic Drivers That Fuel Urban Growth

Jacobs had a unique understanding of the economic forces that drive the growth of cities. Her theories about import replacement as outlined in *The Economy of Cities* accord largely with the nature of the growth that Chinese cities have been experiencing over the past two generations. Jacobs held that through entrepreneurial discovery, local economies figure out ways to deliver goods and services in a more cost-effective manner than the suppliers of the exports they previously relied upon, enjoying regional growth as a result. The manufacture of bicycles is a classic example, with Asian manufacturers taking advantage of lower labor and shipping costs and the enormous local market to produce bikes that are cheaper to manufacture than their European and American counterparts. Today, more than 60 percent of all bicycle parts are manufactured in China.

The proximity of those bicycle manufacturers to one another and the community that developed around them resulted in entrepreneurial spinoffs, including the design and manufacture of internal combustion engines for lawn mowers and motorcycles, and of automobiles, luxury cars, hybrids, and, recently, solar panels and wind turbines. Jacobs recognized that this phenomenon is the primary economic engine behind the growth of cities: Pursuing the initial premise (making cheaper bikes) requires a functional representative government, citywide infrastructure improvements for the movement of people and materials, openness toward the immigration of people with the requisite skills, adequate housing, educational facilities, and other uses that serve cities' populations. These are all related economic drivers that promote regional growth. First and foremost, Jacobs taught us that cities are agglomerations of technically proficient workforces and the urban infrastructures that support them.

## IDENTIFYING THE PRIMARY ROLE OF THE STREET

The second major impact Jacobs had stems from her detailed explanation of how urban blocks and streets interact within the life of the city. Her unique understanding of the complexities and benefits of mixing uses in close proximity was groundbreaking in its time and set the scene for the promotion of greater land-use flexibility and diversity within the fields of planning and urban design. She especially saw diversity as essential to the life of cities, with a mixture of backgrounds, skill sets, and demographics creating the "messy vitality" of an urban neighborhood. Because of this insight, we now have a much more nuanced understanding of how land uses can be blurred and mixed to the great benefit of a community. Concepts such as live/work, flex space, cohousing, and creative mixed use all have their grounding in Jacobs's original thinking on this subject.

Jacobs also had a special understanding of the dynamic between public and private life, and provided valuable insights into the role that street-fronting uses play in the community dynamic. She coined the phrase "eyes on the street" as a way to explain how neighborhoods work in the policing of the public realm and to show how mixed uses interact throughout the day to make the street more vital. Though not a designer, Jacobs understood the physical environment and the duality of the sidewalk's relationship to the street and the building—particularly that sidewalks should offer the flexibility needed for certain uses to "spill out" or engage the public right-of-way, her favorite example being the White Horse Tavern in the West Village. She also understood and explained the street's role not only as a corridor for movement but also as a public space for play and other interactions. This thinking prefigured the recognition of the "third place"—the public right-of-way, which ideally should be used for a variety of activities between work and home in the life of the city.

## PROMOTING PUBLIC ENGAGEMENT

Jacobs has most famously had an impact on the practice of community engagement in the planning process. One of the most powerful portions of *Death and Life* is the first 100 pages, where she takes on the history of the planning profession and critiques its supposed missteps in community engagement, criticizing it as insulated from the communities it serves. She uses this discussion to clear the ground for her primary point: that cities are for people and should be changed only with people's full engagement and informed consent. Jacobs is a hero for insisting upon a more meaningful role for community activism in planning, but it is worth noting that she left New York in part because she became tired of being called upon to fight nearly every city planning initiative after her early success.

Although using community activism to stop ill-advised planning projects from moving forward is a legitimate goal, we must also recognize the time and places in which we live. At the time of writing, polls indicate that only 21 percent of Americans trust the government to do the right thing.[1] This was not always the case, and it certainly is not the case currently in China. Because they have seen significant improvement in their quality of life in the past few generations, the Chinese mostly trust government in matters not related to freedom of speech.[2] I doubt any significant group in China will rise to a point of serious confrontation with the government if the average growth rate continues at the pace it has over the last 20 years.[3] Is there any government-led initiative that can create a more positive fundamental change in the quality of life for the greatest number than job creation?

So one of the issues we should think about in terms of the impact of Jacobs on the profession is how the field of planning is generally perceived in the West, in comparison to how it is seen in the East. As the field of planning is chiefly an institution of the state, it is perceived differently in different cultures, based largely upon the relationship the average citizen might have with his or her government. It is at this point that I would like to compare some of my firm's own experiences in working in China, because I believe they can shed light upon the role of Jacobs's ideas in China's future.

I head a team that is currently working on major redevelopments within major cities in most areas of China. Ten years ago, the largest and most high-profile projects were generally among the cities of the eastern coastline, such as Shanghai, Hong Kong, and Beijing. Today, mainly because of government investment, many significant redevelopment projects are occurring throughout the country. More than 30 cities in China have populations of more than a million, with many considered second- or third-tier cities. In an effort to retain competitiveness, the central government has been careful to spread the wealth and not focus investment just on the top metropolitan markets.

## CASE STUDY 1: GUANGZHOU

Guangzhou is one of the cities that have benefited most from being a special economic zone, which affords companies that do business there special tax breaks. A common recent phenomenon in cities such as Guangzhou is the razing of older worker villages for redevelopment into major mixed use cores. As in Shenzhen, the worker villages in Guangzhou were developed less than two generations, for families relocating from the countryside for factory jobs in the city; and since then, the city has grown up around them. The village site in which we are working contains major stops for subway and bus services. Along the western edge of the site is one of the commercial arterials of the city, providing a significant new address for high-rise office and residential developments. Across the street sits one of the key shopping centers of the region.

The project area, roughly 45 acres or 10 city blocks, is home to some 4,000 residents. Within the village, you will find small concrete-block buildings of mostly residential use. As is typical, there are also well-attended community amenities—a local temple and an elementary school—but by no means is the village adequately served. Within the residential area is a warren of small paved passages between 6 and 15 feet wide; these passages are suitable for pedestrians, bicycles, and scooters, but not automobiles or trucks. Goods transport and garbage removal occur via hand-drawn carts. The residential blocks are made up of walkup-style apartments, typically six to eight stories in height. Demographically, it is not atypical to see three generations living together within a one- or two-room apartment of between 200 and 500 gross square feet. Depending on how long it has been since the family relocated from a rural area, they might also keep a chicken (for fresh eggs) in the apartment.

If the apartment is on the ground floor, the family may have a retail store or provide services to the local community. In my most recent walk through the village, I made a list of the retailers and service providers I could distinguish: cigarette shop, dentist, restaurant, fresh fruit and vegetable vendors, live chicken farmer-butcher, lawn-mower-parts sales, bootleg CD sales, hairdresser, cake decorator, fish market, apparel shops, etc. It was a rainy day, and the fishmonger had strung some freshly caught catfish together and was keeping them alive by letting them swim in the storm gutter. The storefront dentist took a moment from his work extracting a tooth to wave as I walked by.

Obviously, this section of Guangzhou is a place of tremendous diversity and street life. The amount of pedestrian activity through the day and into the night is brisk, and it is clearly a very safe area. And yet unlike the West Village of Jacobs's book, the area is almost completely lacking in basic services; electricity is a snarl of overhead wires, plumbing is unsanitary, and the living conditions are generally one step above squalid, with little charm or bohemian artfulness. The streets look like the famous pictures of Mulberry and Canal streets in New York City taken by social reformer Jacob Riis in the early 1900s. When I ask village residents, they say they would gladly live up above the street in air-conditioned high rises in preference to their current situation, where the air is often overwrought with the sounds and smells of village life.

Our client is a large residential and commercial developer who is in a sole-source negotiation with the city. This developer has the financial wherewithal to buy out each of the villagers at a fair market price, move them out during construction, relocate them into the new development, and allow, where appropriate, local businesses to be relocated. In addition, roughly 35 percent of the site will be dedicated to educational facilities, parks, and open spaces for residents. In exchange, the developer will build at more than twice the current density on the site and double the number of residents, to more than 10,000. The site will also include a significant commercial component, including a partially open-air shopping center, hotel, and office space. Also important to the scheme will be pedestrian connections to the subway station via a major events plaza, which will anchor the site, as well as a network of tree-lined streets with wide sidewalks, street-oriented retail and services, plazas, and pocket parks. A grand public central park, taking up 25 percent of the land area, is proposed for the heart of the scheme. The client told me he has close to 100 percent sign-off on the project from village residents. The total time from master plan concept to the first clearing of the site for development was about half a year. Needless to say, such unanimity and speed are practically unheard of today anywhere in North America. In China, these can be attributed equally to the people's acceptance of change in pursuit of a better quality of life, significant individual compensation, and, yes, a bit of government-imposed fear as well.

## CASE STUDY 2: QINGDAO ECO NEW CAPITAL

The City of Qingdao in northeastern China engaged our firm to create a sustainable master plan for redevelopment of a district in the heart of the city. Having worked in developing countries for a number of years, I have on occasion seen a city embark on a redevelopment project when its country experiences a major success on the world stage. The Qingdao project was driven by the desire of party leaders to make a statement in the wake of the 2008 Olympics in Beijing and the 2010 World Expo in Shanghai.

The site (roughly 1,000 acres) was determined by the central government to be blighted. The local community was a combination of industrial workers and agricultural interests that were using the site for low-value purposes and had been disregarded, by the central government for many years. Because of the site's strategic location, however—central to the Shandong peninsula, fronting a major arterial and transit link between the airport and the downtown—it was full of potential. Each of the landholders was offered an opportunity to participate in the development of the property, either through relocation off the site or through tenancy in the redevelopment, with limitations on use.[4]

As the site is so large, there were many local conditions to address, mitigate, or improve. Many areas of the site had severe air, water, and soil contamination. The plan was driven by the concept of creating a new capital district for Shandong province based upon ecological and economic sustainability principles. Programmatically, the government saw a need for a new administrative center to better serve the area, significant commercial and mixed use areas, new residential neighborhoods, and, taking cues from America, an auto mall—all important future revenue streams for the government. A significant hilltop park existed in the heart of the site but could not easily be accessed from the perimeter, providing little amenity and needing expansion to provide regional connections to the coast. The primary streets bounding the site provided important opportunities for commercial and mixed use growth, along with the need for street improvements and multimodal transit.

I was told by a government official that this project is considered the most important in all of Qingdao (though he did not say by whom). He did assure me that implementation will occur quickly, and it is clear that the development community has quickly fallen into line. Full build-out is projected in about five years, providing new residency to about 150,000 people, hundreds of new commercial uses, and civic activities for the region.

## CASE STUDY 3: DACHONG VILLAGE, SHENZHEN

This project is a 165-acre redevelopment in one of the fastest-growing cities in the world. Planned as a linear city, Shenzhen relies upon an elongated grid of streets that link the city east to west. The site is on the western edge, along the major bridge connection to Hong Kong. As such, it is a very important gateway to the city. The government saw an opportunity to create a redevelopment site out of the Dachong neighborhood, whose developments, created just two generations ago, are now significantly blighted. The site is filled with six- to eight-story walkup apartment buildings with local shopping on the ground floors. Several temples, significant trees, and a large man-made reservoir offer unique features for preservation and integration into the plan, but serious overcrowding, poor living conditions, and antiquated infrastructure prevail. Most of the 6,000 residents had long-term leases from the government, and part of the provision of the release of the land for redevelopment was that there had to be significant approval by residents of the design. What percentage of the population "significant" represented was not divulged.

The plan was developed over the span of about six months. An international competition was held, and the residents had a say about which consultant was selected from the numerous entries; however, by no means were they the primary decision makers. The development program was proposed by the developer: a density at close to five times the existing one, consisting of mostly residential development, with significant office, retail, hotel, and civic uses. The density will add 60,000 new residents to the area (a huge number)—but the development will also provide much-needed improvements to the local infrastructure, add schools and play areas, provide thousands of local jobs, and replace all of the housing and shop space of the existing village while also providing relocation stipends for all who leave, voluntarily or otherwise.

Interestingly, Shenzhen is the youngest of the three cities outlined here, but it has enjoyed a relatively long period of significant redevelopment growth and has a rapidly growing middle class. Perhaps as a result, the community was much more involved in decision making than in the other two case studies. After selection, the plan was refined to better address the villagers' needs in terms of location within the plan, types of storefronts and open spaces, locations and configurations of nearby amenities, and types of residential offerings. A deadline for signing onto the project plan was enforced by the developer, with financial incentives for those who participated. I am told by the developer that, to date, 98 percent of the villagers have opted into the project. The rest are to be quietly incentivized through a combination of private sector and government intervention. This is in practice not dissimilar to American redevelopment precedent, where agencies pay fair market value and bear relocation costs for residents and businesses affected by redevelopment initiatives. The significant difference is the long legal precedent for such actions in the United States, whereas in China a private citizen has limited, if any, legal recourse.

## CONCLUSION

In all of these cases, the economic opportunities for redevelopment, the grand aspirations for each site set forth by planners, and the developers' desire to mold the right project for the market trumped most other concerns. What differed among these cases was the level of each community's ability to negotiate the precise terms of each redevelopment. Jane Jacobs might have appreciated the local forces of economic development and the prosperity it might foster, but she also might have seen a vast manipulated populace that cannot significantly shape its own environment in any significant way.

In early 2010, the *New York Times* published a front-page article on the state of Chinese real estate.[5] The reporters described an overheated market in which redevelopment and land sales are the primary drivers of many local economies; in some areas, real estate transactions account for up to 60 percent of local government revenue. They wrote of disempowered residents frustrated by not having a say in the future of their communities, forced out of their homes without equitable compensation for their relocation, resorting to ugly clashes—in some cases self-immolation—in protest. "Powerless to stay and too poor to move, many Chinese have rebelled. 'Nail houses'—homes sticking out on tracts of cleared land, whose owners resist eviction—are common. So are tales of corruption and other abuses." The article went on to describe the Chinese real estate marketplace as an ongoing land grab, with city officials in cahoots with developers to level and remake entire swaths of older sections of cities, with little or no interaction with local residents, to meet a seemingly endless need for new housing.

How accurate is this view? Are the Chinese people being exploited to the degree described? If so, is Jane Jacobs a source of inspiration for the disenfranchised in China?

Most government-funded redevelopments are fueled to a greater or lesser degree by a combination of three factors that we can relate, positively or negatively, to Jacobs's areas of influence: (1) the competitive economic advantage that China currently enjoys in the marketplace, which creates a tremendous demand for housing and commercial growth within urban centers; (2) a growing middle class, exposed to better education and travel opportunities, which fuels demand for a more modern and sophisticated style of life; and (3) a visionary and stable political system with leaders who aspire to show new thinking and global leadership in the essential matters of urban life.

It is safe to say Jacobs is being rediscovered as someone who understood the life and glory of cities on their experiential merits, rather than commercial means alone. As in North America, her ideas are most fully embraced in those urban areas where a sense of history and urban pastiche is most greatly developed—Shanghai, Hangzhou, Beijing, Hong Kong, and perhaps a few other places. We in North America now work with a mind toward Jacobs's understanding of the city as a series of interconnected experiences that can be woven into a compelling narrative. Her understanding of the city was sequential, emotional, and cinematic. To her, the city told a million stories, played out in all their drama on the sidewalks. Her sense of narrative is a powerful tool for interpreting the existing city in modern planning practice. Jacobs had an intuitive knowledge that the urban experience is a layered one, full of many uses and histories. Inventory and preservation of not only historic buildings but also neighborhoods is now common practice.

In regard to the premise of discovering the essential role of the street, in China that role is currently colored by some fundamental challenges. In many cities, the street's current iteration often includes odd adjacencies and discordance. The fishmonger in Guangzhou reminded me of some our landmark property decisions, including the Supreme Court's *Euclid v. Ambler*, in which industrial uses were deemed inappropriate for a residential area, resulting in the beginning of modern zoning. Despite the passing of about 100 years and the significant geographic distance, the same issue exists in modern China. Sometimes government intervention through good planning is the only way out of a difficult situation before nuanced appreciation can occur.

As always, the history of cities is a dynamic between growth and prosperity on one side and preservation on the other. Jacobs's work is important because it presented two not necessarily conflicting views of the city: one ruled by markets and competitive advantage in *The Economy of Cities*, and the other ruled by community values in *Death and Life*. Both books see the true value of cities in modern life from different perspectives, but both present a fundamental understanding of the positive influence that urbanism has made to our way of life.

Outsiders often point to the lack of public dialogue in China as a lack of human rights. While there is truth to this, it is also true that many Chinese retain a sincere optimism and trust in their public systems as stewards of the future, which Westerners rarely have anymore. The community activism that was so effective in stopping Robert Moses's more extreme plans was more a reflection of revealing his reckless ambition than it was a proper appreciation of the ability of planning to effect change for the greater good. Planning considerations such as environmental stewardship, job creation, social equity, adequate infrastructure, and high-quality public services are still significant challenges of our era. The soaring accomplishments of the planning profession (such as the Plan of Chicago, Boston's Emerald Necklace, the Beijing Olympics, and Malmö, Sweden) show that big thinking is often essential to bring about fundamental change for the better in our modern cities. If she came to China with me and saw these projects I described, in all their complexity, I am sure Jane Jacobs would understand that the good in large-scale planning is not necessarily outweighed by the bad. And, if she is credited with spurring the movement that led to greater citizen participation in development and planning decisions, is it legitimate for us to wonder if we have, in the process, unintentionally yet fundamentally weakened our ability to do grandly ambitious projects in North America?

# Jane Jacobs and the Death and Life of American Planning

## Thomas J. Campanella

And the end of all our exploring
Will be to arrive where we started
And know the place for the first time.
T. S. Eliot, "Little Gidding"

During a recent departmental retreat here at the University of North Carolina at Chapel Hill, planning faculty conducted a brainstorming session in which each professor—including me—was asked to list, anonymously on a bit of paper, some of the major issues and concerns facing the profession today. These lists were then collected and transcribed on the whiteboard. All the expected big themes were there—sustainability and global warming, equity and justice, peak oil, immigration, urban sprawl and public health, retrofitting suburbia, and so on. But also on the board appeared, like a sacrilegious graffito, the words "Trivial Profession."[1] When we then voted to rank the listed items in order of importance, "Trivial Profession" was placed—lo and behold—close to the top. This surprised and alarmed a number of people in the room. Here were members of one of the finest planning faculties in America, at one of the most respected programs in the world, suggesting that their chosen field was minor and irrelevant.

Now, even the most parochial among us would probably agree that urban planning is not one of society's bedrock professions, such as law or medicine or perhaps economics. It is indeed a minor field, and that's fine. Nathan Glazer, in his well-known essay "Schools of the Minor Professions," labeled "minor" *every* profession outside law and medicine. Not even clerics or divines made his cut. Moreover, Glazer observed that attempts on the part of "occupations" such as urban planning to transform themselves "into professions in the older sense, and the assimilation of their programmes of training into academic institutions, have not gone smoothly."[2] But minority status by itself is not why "Trivial Profession" appeared on the whiteboard. It was there because of a swelling perception, especially among young scholars and practitioners, that planning is a diffuse and ineffective field, and that it has been largely unsuccessful over the last half century at its own game: bringing about more just, sustainable, healthful, efficient, and beautiful cities and urban regions. It was there because of a looming sense that planners in America simply lack the agency or authority to turn their idealism into reality, that planning has neither the prestige nor the street cred necessary to effect real and lasting change.

To understand the roots of this sense of impotence and ennui requires us to dial back to the great cultural shift that occurred in the planning field beginning in the 1960s. The seeds of discontent sown in that era brought forth new and needed growth, which nonetheless choked out three vital aspects of the planning profession—its *disciplinary identity*, *professional authority*, and *visionary capacity*. I'll address each aspect in turn before tackling the messy but urgent matter of their recovery in this age of unprecedented challenge to the planning profession worldwide.

It is well known that city planning in the United States evolved out of the landscape architectural profession during the late Olmsted era. Planning's core expertise was then grounded and tangible. It was chiefly concerned with accommodating human needs and functions on the land, from the scale of the site to that of entire regions. One of the founders of the Chapel Hill program, F. Stuart Chapin Jr. (whose first degree was in architecture), described planning as "a means for systematically anticipating and achieving adjustment in the physical environment of a city consistent with social and economic trends and sound principles of civic design."[3] The goal was to create physical settings that would help bring about a more prosperous, efficient, and equitable society. And in many ways the giants of the prewar planning profession—Olmsted Jr., Burnham, Mumford, Stein and Wright, Nolen, and Gilmore D. Clarke—were successful in doing just that.

The postwar period was something else altogether. By then, middle-class Americans were buying cars and moving to the suburbs in record numbers. The urban core was slowly being depopulated. Cities were losing their tax base, buildings were being abandoned, and neighborhoods were falling victim to blight. Planners and civic leaders were increasingly desperate to save their cities. Help came soon enough from Uncle Sam. Passage of the 1949 Housing Act, with its infamous Title I proviso, made urban renewal a legitimate target for federal funding. Flush with cash, city redevelopment agencies commissioned urban planners to prepare slum-clearance master plans. Vibrant ethnic neighborhoods—including the one my mother grew up in near the Brooklyn Navy Yard—were blotted out by Voisinian superblocks or punched through with expressways meant to make downtown easily accessible to suburbanites. Urban planners in the postwar period thus aided and abetted some of the most egregious acts of urban vandalism in American history. Of course, they did not see it this way. Most believed, like Lewis Mumford, that America's cities were suffering an urban cancer wholly untreatable by the home remedies Jane Jacobs was brewing and that the strong medicine of slum clearance was just what the doctor ordered. Like their architect colleagues, postwar planners had drunk the Corbusian Kool-Aid and were too intoxicated to see the terrible harm they were causing.

Thus ensued the well-deserved backlash against superblock urbanism and the authoritarian, we-experts-know-best brand of planning that backed it. And the backlash came, of course, from a bespectacled young journalist named Jane Jacobs. Her 1961 *The Death and Life of Great American Cities*, much like the paperwork Luther nailed to the Schlosskirche Wittenberg four centuries earlier, sparked a reformation—this time within the planning profession. To the rising generation of planners, coming of age in an era of cultural ferment and rebellion against the status quo, Jane Jacobs was a patron saint. The young idealists soon set about rewiring the planning field. The ancien régime was put on trial for failures real and imagined, for not responding adequately to the impending urban crisis, and especially for ignoring issues of urban poverty and racial discrimination. But change did not come easily; the field was plunged into disarray. A glance at the July 1970 issue of the *Journal of the American Institute of Planners* (precursor to

*JAPA*) reveals a profession gripped by a crisis of mission, purpose, and relevance. As the authors of one article—fittingly titled "Holding Together"—asked, how could this well-meaning discipline transform itself "against a background of trends in the society and the profession that invalidate many of the assumptions underlying traditional planning education"?[4]

One way was to disgorge itself of the muscular physical-interventionist focus that had long been planning's métier. King Laius was thus slain by Oedipus, in love with "Mother Jacobs," as Mumford derisively called her.[5] Forced from his lofty perch, the once-mighty planner now found himself in a hot and crowded city street. No longer would he twirl a compass above the city like a conductor's baton, as did the anonymous planner depicted on a first-day cover for the 1967 stamp Plan for Better Cities (he even wears a pinky ring!). So thoroughly internalized was the Jacobs critique that planners could see only folly and failure in the work of their own professional forebears. Burnham's grand dictum "Make no little plans" went from a battle cry to an embarrassment in less than a decade. Even so revered and saintly a figure as Sir Ebenezer Howard was now a pariah. Jacobs herself described the good man—one of the great progressives of the late Victorian era—as a mere "court reporter," a clueless amateur who yearned "to do the city in" with "powerful and city-destroying ideas."[6] Indeed, to Jacobs, not just misguided American urban renewal but the entire enterprise of visionary, rational, centralized planning was foul and suspect. She was as opposed to new towns as she was to inner-city slum clearance—anything that threatened the vitality and sustenance of traditional urban forms was the enemy. It is largely forgotten that the popular United Kingdom edition of *Death and Life* was subtitled "The Failure of Town Planning." How odd that such a conservative, even reactionary, stance would galvanize an entire generation of planners.

The Jacobsians sought fresh methods of making cities work—from the grassroots and the bottom up. The subaltern was exalted, the master laid low. The drafting tables were tossed for pickets and surveys and spreadsheets. Planners sought new alliances in academe, beyond the schools of architecture and design—in political science, law, economics, sociology, and so forth. But there were problems. First, none of the social sciences were themselves primarily concerned with the city, and so at best they could be only partial allies. Second, planning was not taken seriously by any of these fields. The schoolboy crush was not returned, making the relationship unequal from the start. Even today it's rare for a social science department to hire a planning Ph.D., while planning programs routinely hire academics with doctorates in economics, political science, and other fields. Indeed, Nathan Glazer observed that one of the hallmarks of a minor profession is that faculty with "outside" doctorates actually enjoy *higher prestige* within the field than those with degrees in the profession itself.[7] They also tend to have minimal allegiance to planning. As William Rich observed of the Massachusetts Institute of Technology faculty in the 1970s, members "from outside often tended to identify more strongly with their professional colleagues in other departments and schools than with the planning staff."[8]

This brings us to the first of the three legacies of the Jacobsian turn: *It diminished the disciplinary identity of the planning profession.* While the expanded range of planning scholarship and practice in the post–urban renewal era diversified the field, that diversification came at the expense of an established area of expertise—strong, centralized physical planning—that gave the profession visibility and identity both within academia and among sibling "place" professions such as architecture and landscape architecture. My students are always astonished to learn just how toxic and stigmatized physical planning—today one of the most popular concentrations in many programs—had become by the 1970s. Like a well-meaning surgeon who botches an operation, planners were (correctly) blamed for the excesses of urban renewal and many other problems then facing American cities. But the planning baby was thrown out with the urban-renewal bathwater. And once the traditional focus of physical planning was lost, the profession was effectively without a keel. It became fragmented and balkanized, which has since created a kind of chronic identity crisis within the field—a nagging uncertainty about purpose and relevance. Certainly in the popular imagination, physical planning was what planners did—they choreographed the buildings and infrastructure on the land. By the mid-1970s, however, even educated laypersons would have difficulty understanding what the profession was all about. Today, planners *themselves* often have a hard time explaining the purpose of their profession. By forgoing its traditional focus and expanding too quickly, planning became a jack-of-all-trades, master of none. And so it remains.

The second legacy of the Jacobsian revolution is closely related to the first: *Privileging the grassroots over plannerly authority and expertise meant a loss of professional agency.*

In rejecting the muscular interventionism of the Burnham-Moses sort, planners in the 1960s identified instead with the victims of urban renewal and highway schemes. New mechanisms were devised to empower ordinary citizens and the grassroots to shape and guide the planning process. This was an extraordinary act of altruism on our part, and I can think of no other profession that has done anything quite like it. Imagine economists at the Federal Reserve holding community meetings and polls to decide the direction of fiscal policy. Imagine public health officials giving equal weight to the nutritional wisdom of teenagers— they are stakeholders, after all! Granted, powering up the grassroots was necessary in the 1970s to stop expressway and renewal schemes that had truly run amok. But it was power that could not easily be switched off. Tools and processes introduced to ensure popular participation ended up reducing the planner's role to that of umpire or schoolyard monitor. Instead of setting the terms of debate or charting a course of action, planners now seemed wholly content to be facilitators—"mere *absorbers* of public opinion," as Alex Krieger put it, "waiting for consensus to build."[9]

The fatal flaw of such populism is that no single group of local citizens—mainstream or marginalized, affluent or impoverished—can be trusted to have the best interests of society or the environment in mind when they evaluate a planning proposal. The literature on grassroots planning tends to assume a citizenry of Gandhian humanists. In fact, most people are not motivated by altruism or yearning for a better world but by self-interest, pure and simple. Preservation and enhancement of that self-interest—which usually orbits about the axes of rising crime rates and falling property values—are the real drivers of community activism. This is why it is a fool's errand to rely upon citizens to guide the planning process. Forget for a moment that most folks lack the knowledge and expertise to make intelligent decisions about the future of our cities. Most people are too busy, too apathetic, or too focused on their jobs or kids to be moved to action over planning issues unless those issues are at their doorstep. And once an issue is at the doorstep, fear sets in and reason and rationality fly out the window. So the very citizens least able to make objective decisions about planning action are the ones who end up dominating the planning process, often wielding near-veto power over proposals.

To be fair, activism of the NIMBY sort is a fierce guard dog that's helped put an end to some very bad projects, by the private sector as well as the government. And there are times when citizen self-interest and the greater social good do overlap. In Orange County, North Carolina, part of the Research Triangle and home to Chapel Hill, grassroots activism put an end to a proposed asphalt plant and stopped the North Carolina Department of Transportation's dreams of a six-lane bypass that would have ruined a pristine forest tract along the Eno River. But the same community activism has also canceled several proposed infill projects, thus helping drive development to rural greenfield sites. (Cows are slow to organize.) It's made the Orange County homeless shelter homeless itself, almost ended a proposed Habitat for Humanity housing complex in Chapel Hill, and generated opposition to a much-needed transit-oriented development in the county seat of Hillsborough (more on this in a moment). And for what it's worth, the shrillest opposition in each of these cases came not from rednecks or Tea Party activists but from highly educated "creative class" progressives who effectively weaponized Jane Jacobs to oppose anything they perceived as threatening the status quo—including projects that would reduce our carbon footprint, create more affordable housing, and shelter the homeless.

NIMBYism has been described as "the bitter fruit of a pluralistic democracy in which all views carry equal weight."[10] And that, sadly, includes the voice of the planner. In the face of an aroused and angry public, plannerly wisdom and expertise have no more clout than the ranting of the loudest community activist; and this is both wrong and a hazard to our collective future. For who, if not the planner, will advocate on behalf of society at large? All planning may be local, but the sum of the local is national and eventually global. If we put parochial local interests ahead of broader societal needs, it will be impossible to build the infrastructure essential to the economic viability of the United States in the long haul—the commuter and high-speed rail lines; the dense, walkable, public-transit-focused communities; the solar and wind farms and geothermal plants; perhaps even the nuclear power stations.

The third legacy of the Jacobsian turn is perhaps most troubling of all: *the seeming paucity among American planners today of the speculative courage and vision that once distinguished this profession.* I'll ease into this subject by way of a story—one that will appear to contradict some of what I just wrote about citizen-led planning.

I have served for several years now on the planning board of Hillsborough, North Carolina, where my wife and I have lived since 2004. Hillsborough, founded in 1754, is a charming little town some 10 miles north of Chapel Hill. It's always reminded me of a smaller, grittier, less precious version of Concord, Massachusetts. It has a long and rich history, progressive leadership, and an arts and culture scene many times its size. It is also blessed with a palpable genius loci: "If there are hot spots on the globe, as the ancients believed," writes resident Frances Mayes, author of *Under the Tuscan Sun*, "Hillsborough must be one of them."[11] The town is also located on one of the main rail arteries in the South, and has been since the Civil War. Every day several Amtrak trains—including the Carolinian, the fastest-growing passenger line in the United States—speed through town on their way to Charlotte or Raleigh, North Carolina, Washington, D.C., and New York. But a passenger train hasn't made a scheduled stop in Hillsborough since March 1964, when Southern Railway ended service due to declining ridership. After a century of connectivity, Hillsborough and Orange County were cut loose from the nation's rail grid.

In late 2007 a group of residents in our local coffee shop, a classic Oldenburg "third place" named Cup-A-Joe, got to talking about reviving rail service. Soon a petition was drafted, and within a few months several hundred people had signed it.[12] At the same time, I had students in my urban design and site planning class develop conceptual schemes for a station-anchored mixed use development on land along the tracks close to downtown. I invited town officials to the final review. The local newspaper did an article. Six months later the town purchased the parcel and set about appointing a task force to explore plans for a station. Amtrak, unprompted, produced a study showing that a Hillsborough stop would be profitable. The North Carolina Railroad Company, owner of the right-of-way and long a Kafka's Castle of impenetrability, suddenly got interested. Task-force members were treated to a corridor tour in the railroad's track-riding

Chevy Suburban; we were invited to conferences and seminars. The North Carolina Department of Transportation eventually submitted a request on our behalf for funding from the American Recovery and Reinvestment Act. The station was, after all, a poster child for the sort of infrastructure project President Obama's stimulus package was ostensibly intended to support.

And all along I kept wondering: "Why did this have to come out of a coffee shop and a classroom? *Where were the planne*rs? Why didn't the town or county planning office act on this opportunity at its doorstep?" A moment ago I argued that the public lacks the knowledge and expertise to make informed decisions about city planning. If that's the case, what does it say about our profession when a group of citizens—most with no training whatsoever in architecture, planning, or design—comes up with a very good idea *that the planners should have had*? When I asked about this, the response was: "We're too busy planning to come up with big plans."[13] Too busy planning. Too busy slogging through the bureaucratic maze, issuing permits and enforcing zoning codes, hosting community get-togethers, making sure developers get their submittals in on time and pay their fees. This is what passes for planning today. We have become a caretaker profession—reactive rather than proactive, corrective instead of preemptive, rule bound and hamstrung and anything but visionary. If we lived in Nirvana, this would be fine. But we don't. We are entering the uncharted waters of urbanization on a scale the world has never seen. And we are not in the wheelhouse, let alone steering the ship. We may not even be on board.

How did this come about? How did a profession that roared to life with such grand ambitions become such a mouse? The answer points to the self-inflicted loss of agency and authority that came with the Jacobs revolution. It's hard to be a visionary when you've divested yourself of the power to turn visions into reality. Planning in America has been reduced to smallness and timidity, and largely by its own hand. So it's no surprise that envisioning alternative futures for our cities and towns and regions has defaulted to non-planners such as William McDonough and Richard Florida, Andrés Duany and Rem Koolhaas, and journalists such as Joel Kotkin and the inimitable James Howard Kunstler. Jane Jacobs was just the start. It is almost impossible to name a single urban planner today who is a regular presence on the editorial pages of a major newspaper, who has galvanized popular sentiment on issues such as sprawl and peak oil, or who has published a best-selling book on the great issues of our day in this age of unprecedented global urbanization. We are the presumptive stewards of the urban future, yet we have ceded the charting of our very own field to others.

Late in life, even Jane Jacobs grew frustrated with the timidity and lack of imagination on the part of planners—Canadian planners this time. In an April 1993 speech—later published in the *Ontario Planning Journal*—she lamented the *absence* of just the sort of robust plannerly interventionism that she once condemned. Jacobs read through a long list of exemplary planning initiatives—the Toronto Main Street effort; the new Planning for Ontario guidelines; efforts to plan the Toronto waterfront; and plans for infill housing in the city, the renewal and extension of streetcar transit, the redevelopment of the St. Lawrence downtown neighborhood, and on and on. And then she unleashed this bitter missile: "Not one of these forward-looking and important policies and ideas—not ONE—was the intellectual product of an official planning department, whether in Toronto, Metro, or the province." Indeed, she drove on, "our official planning departments seem to be brain-dead in the sense that we cannot depend on them in any way, shape, or form for providing intellectual leadership in addressing urgent problems involving the physical future of the city." This, I hardly need to add, from a person who did more than any other to quash plannerly agency to shape the physical city.[14]

Well, what can be done about all this? And what might the doing mean for the future of planning education? How can we cultivate in planners the kind of bold visionary thinking that characterized this profession in its youth? How can we ensure that the enthusiasm and bright-eyed idealism so typical of our students is not extinguished as they move into the world of practice? How can we transform planners into big-picture thinkers with the speculative courage to imagine alternatives to the urban status quo, and equipped with the skills and the moxie required to lead the recovery of American infrastructure and put the nation on a greener, more sustainable path?

As I've argued throughout this chapter, it was the Jacobsian revolution and its elimination of a robust physical-planning focus that led to the diminution of planning's disciplinary identity, professional agency, and speculative courage. Thus I believe that a renewed emphasis on physical planning—the grounded, tangible, place-bound matter of orchestrating human activity on the land—is essential to refocusing, recalibrating, and renewing the planning profession in America. By this I do not mean regression back to the state of affairs circa 1935. Planning prior to the grassroots revolution was indeed shallow and undisciplined in many respects. Most of what was embraced post-Jacobs must remain—our expertise on public policy and economics, on law and governance and international development, on planning process and community involvement, on hazard mitigation and environmental impact, on ending poverty and creating cities of justice and equality. But all these areas of concern should be subordinated to a core set of competencies related to placemaking, infrastructure, and the physical environment, both built and natural. I am not suggesting that we simply toss in a few studio courses and call it a day. Planners should certainly be versed in key theories of landscape and urban design. But more than design skills are needed if planning is to become—as I feel it must—the charter discipline and conscience of the placemaking professions in coming decades.

Planning students today need a more robust suite of skills and expertise than we are currently providing—and than may even be possible in the framework of the two-year graduate curriculum.[15] Planners today need not a close-up lens or a wide-angle lens but a wide-angle zoom lens. They need to be able to see the big picture as well as the parts close up; and even if they are not trained to design the parts themselves, they need to know how all those parts fit together. They need, as Jerold Kayden has put it, to "understand, analyze, and influence the variety of forces—social, economic, cultural, legal, political, ecological, technological, aesthetic, and so forth—shaping the built environment."[16] This means that in addition to being taught courses in economics and law and governance, planning students should be trained to be keen observers of the urban landscapes about them, to be able to decipher the riddles of architectural style and substance, to have a working knowledge of the historical development of places and patterns on the land. They should understand how the physical infrastructure of a city works—the mechanics of transportation and utility systems, sewerage, and water supply. They should know the fundamentals of ecology and the natural systems of a place, be able to read a site and its landform and vegetation, know that a great spreading maple in the middle of a stand of pines once stood alone in an open pasture. They need to know the basics of impact analysis and be able to assess the implications of a proposed development on traffic, water quality, and a city's carbon footprint. And while they cannot master all of site engineering, they should be competent site analysts and—more important—be fluent in assessing the site plans of others. Such training would place competency in the shaping and stewardship of the built environment at the very center of the planning-education solar system. And about that good sun a multitude of bodies—planning specialties as we have long had them—could happily orbit.

We are far from this ideal today. As it stands, a planning student can get through most graduate programs in the United States without taking a single course in land-use or physical planning. It is fully possible to earn a master's degree at our top planning schools without knowing how to read a contour map, without understanding what a figure-ground drawing represents, without being able to assess the design quality of a storm-water system on a set of plans, without knowing that L'Enfant's design for Washington, D.C., drew from a tradition extending back to 16th-century Rome. This is expertise that was once well covered by required course work in nearly every program. But as planning moved away from its roots, the core of required courses was slowly chiseled away until only a shell remained—and a disputed one at that. So severe was planning's post-Jacobs identity crisis that in the 1970s MIT—then, as now, the premier American program—eliminated *all* required courses for a time. As William Rich observed at the time, few students registered for "subjects related to physical planning or planning fundamentals," while more took courses "in social planning and in other departments." He continued:

> This trend first made itself felt in 1967 when students demand-
> ed, and the faculty agreed, that studio courses be made optional; a
> year later students suggested that all formal course requirements

for the MCP [master's of city planning] degree be eliminated, extending a policy already in use in the doctoral program. Rather than redefine a professional program that would take into account the relevance of research and knowledge from other fields, the faculty eliminated the specific guidelines they had helped make obsolete. They substituted general guidelines intended to accomplish the same result, but even these have been largely ignored by some students and their advisors.

Thus, observed Rich, "as the range of Departmental interests" widened, it became "increasingly difficult to identify substantive areas that ought to concern all students."[17] This essential problem remains. The overextended, unfocused nature of planning today is reflected in a required core of course work so stripped down and minimized that it can hardly stand on its own. Compare this to the way physicians are educated. At medical school and during their residencies, all physicians—regardless of eventual specialization—have to master the basics of internal medicine. They may become psychiatrists or proctologists or cardiac surgeons, but they'll always share a set of core skills that, in the end, define what it is to be a physician. If someone collapses clutching their abdomen in a crowded restaurant, nobody calls for a gastroenterologist; they ask, "Is there a *doctor* in the house?"

Although I know of no program today without required course work of some kind, in most the core is only a shadow of what it once was. At the University of North Carolina, for example, students must take courses in quantitative analysis, economics, planning theory, and urban spatial structure, along with a two-day geographic information systems workshop. But compare this to the requirements for the 1958–1959 academic year. Then, students were all required to take a staggering 13 courses—equivalent to practically the entire curriculum in most programs today. These included Traffic and Transportation, Municipal Facilities and Management, Site Planning, Community Design, Urban Planning Practice, Methods and Techniques, Advanced Planning Design, and an Urban Renewal Seminar. Even a decade later, there were nine required core courses, still with a strong focus on physical planning and environmental design. And this in a program that had never been part of a design school, that was launched from within the sociology department, and that has ever since been a unit in the College of Arts and Sciences.[18]

All this would be academic, literally, were it not for the momentous changes under way in the United States and the world today—changes that will increasingly demand a new level of engaged action on the part of the planning profession. The rapid urbanization of Asia, Africa, and parts of South America is dramatically altering global flows of labor, capital, energy, and natural resources. "Over the next two decades," writes Richard Dobbs, "the world will see a burst of urban expansion at a speed and on a scale never before witnessed in human history."[19] We in the United States face a somewhat opposite conundrum—that of a nation not urbanized enough to be sustainable in the long haul. Planning in America has its work cut out for it as never before: It must take the lead in changing our patterns of settlement on the land, building the necessary infrastructure to end our catastrophic addiction to cheap oil, and working toward a more sustainable urban future. We need to literally come together in space, retrofit suburbia and create dense walkable communities, and build "a country of cities."[20] We need to restore the vast railroads that scored this country a century ago and commit far more federal funding toward rebuilding our bridges and tunnels, our water and sewer infrastructure, our electrical grids. We have coasted for decades on infrastructure built generations ago. That infrastructure served admirably, but it is aging and beginning to fail. How well we respond to these signal challenges will determine whether we are indeed a relevant and important profession or a truly minor one.

The whole matter of planning, infrastructure, and the fate of nations has come into high relief in recent years with the rise of China. Le Corbusier famously observed that to send a young architect to Rome was to ruin him for life. American planners who travel to China risk coming back equally ruined, for they learn that their Chinese cousins have effectively charted the most spectacular period of urban growth and transformation in world history. They are then beset with an affliction far worse than the "Robert Moses envy" suffered, usually in silence, by an earlier generation of American planners. Here now is a nation that makes even Moses look small. Name any category of infrastructure and China has likely built more of it in the last 30 years, and bigger and faster, than any other nation on Earth—probably than all other nations *combined*. Long the poor man of Asia, China is now beating us at a game we once mastered—the game of building, and building big; the game of getting things done.

This envy is spiked, of course, by a growing awareness that China's uncanny ability to build—and our seeming incapacity to do very much at all—is not historically neutral or politically inert but has vast implications for the future viability, competitiveness, and security of the United States. What does it say about a nation that, for example, takes seven years to build a pedestrian footbridge over an expressway in Durham, North Carolina? Seven years! My wife, who grew up in China, finds this astonishing. "But Americans put a man on the moon!" she says. "Seven years to build a little bridge?" Seven years in China means entire new cities built from scratch. It will mean, seven years hence, the most extensive national high-speed rail network on the planet. Already Chinese trains are the fastest in the world. They make the lovely Amtrak Acela—the speediest thing we have—look like it's standing still (which too often it is). Very soon rail travel between Shanghai and Beijing, long an overnight trip, will be down to a mere four hours. Service like that along the U.S. eastern seaboard would mean Boston to New York, or New York to Washington, in just over an hour. Meanwhile, in Raleigh, North Carolina, months have been wasted as citizens, planners, and politicians quarrel over a handful of backyards and parking lots that may get clipped by the proposed Southeast High Speed Rail. And where the United States has earmarked all of $8 billion for high-speed rail, China has allocated $300 billion for phase one alone.

Of course, there are immense equity and justice and environmental issues with the way cities are built and rebuilt in China; we all know that. People are shunted around like so many scared sheep, evicted with only a few weeks' notice. Those who protest are silenced quickly, often violently. I am not advocating the sort of ruthless authoritarian approach to urban growth and renewal that China favors. But just as China needs more of the American-style gavel of justice, equity, and democratic process, we in the United States need more of that very effective Chinese sledgehammer. And this will require something that makes many people nervous: ridding the development process of some of the many trammels and fetters that came in the wake of the Jacobsian grass-roots revolution. For example, community consent is usually an asset to smart planning, but it must be regulated to prevent populist opposition to projects that promise clear benefits to a majority of citizens beyond the local scene.

Think of the infamous Cape Wind project in Massachusetts—the pioneering offshore wind farm venture that was stalled for nearly a decade by an elite minority whose "right project in the wrong place" catchphrase was but a white-wine version of the beer-and-pretzels "not in my backyard." Ten years and 100,000 pages of administrative review later, the visionary project is only now finally nearing construction. The Cape Wind story also highlights the need for much greater elasticity in terms of environmental compliance and mitigation. Here again we have too much of a good thing, where China has not nearly enough. Too-numerous, too-strict environmental laws are often the lever by which development opponents bring good, necessary projects to their knees. Do we really need, for example, a 3-foot stack of environmental impact statements for a single segment of a high-speed rail line on the eastern seaboard? At what point does guardianship of the public interest become obstructionism, a drag on our ability to get anything done at all and thus a hazard to our future? Indeed, if today's requirements for environmental impact assessment—not to mention public comment and review—were in place in the 1930s, only a very tiny fraction of New Deal public works would have been built.

And this brings me to my final point. We can envy China's ability to get things done, but we have a more proximate—and more balanced and equitable—model of our own to look to for inspiration: that heroic era of public works our grandparents orchestrated about 75 years ago, with a fraction of the wealth and twice the Depression we have now. The New Deal, with its storied programs such as the Works Progress Administration and the Civilian Conservation Corp, was American planning's finest hour. The sheer scope and scale of projects built in those otherwise grim years staggers the imagination—Hoover Dam; the Triborough Bridge; the Blue Ridge Parkway; entire state park systems; thousands of schools, libraries, and hospitals; the rural American electric grid; the Tennessee Valley Authority. These are improvements that millions of Americans enjoy and use to this day. Getting such a vast program of works built in less than a decade required a muscular federal government with deep pockets and broad powers of eminent domain. It also required a citizenry willing to accept a certain degree of sacrifice for the good of society and the benefit of the future.

The impediments to a public-works campaign of such scale and ambition today are vast and daunting. Mustering the political will alone would likely be impossible barring an economic meltdown even more severe than the one we are currently mired in. Many Americans—perhaps even a majority—simply don't believe in the ability of the federal government to solve problems anymore. We also no longer have the shared set of norms and values—about nation, about the public realm—necessary to agree upon a bold course of government action. America has always been a nation of freedom-loving individualists. But in the past, primacy of the individual was tempered by common culture. Self-interest was, in effect, harnessed productively to the wagon of collective good. The United States prior to the 1960s was, of course, a far less polyglot society than it is today; consensus formed more easily on many issues. The cultural revolutions of the 1960s brought civil rights to African Americans and others long marginalized by America's white, northern European, Protestant charter culture. But the 1960s—and the "me" decade that followed—also inadvertently unhitched the horses of self-interest from the good cart Commonweal. A new emphasis on cultural relativism made the harmless trope of the American melting pot suddenly toxic. What shared values and mores we once had slowly faded. The incredible diversity of America today—ethnic, religious, cultural, political—is one of our greatest strengths; we are a mighty mirror of the globe itself. But the absence of cultural hegemony also makes it very difficult to reach consensus on anything. If we share no common culture beyond that of consumerism, then we are just so many free-floating, self-interested atoms each seeking its own best orbit.

It goes without saying that an atomized nation of self-serving individuals is not one likely to have much faith in a shared civic realm. Both sides of the political aisle are to blame here. From the right comes peevish insistence on private enterprise and personal liberty at all costs; from the left, a welfare-state culture that has created a generation of Americans expecting handouts like spoiled children. The right is against stimulus spending of any sort; the left seems more eager to spend on public-sector entitlement programs than on public works. Either way, it is the *civitas* that suffers. The American Recovery and Reinvestment Act exemplifies the stalemate. Many observers, including me, were greatly cheered when President Obama signed the so-called Recovery Act into law on February 17, 2009. At first flush it looked very much like the start of the second New Deal, a bold new era of public works, of Americans in shirtsleeves building the parks and power dams of tomorrow. Sadly, it's been nothing of the sort. Of the nearly $790 billion authorized by the stimulus package, a mere $105 billion was tagged for infrastructure, and only a fraction of that for truly progressive plays such as high-speed rail. More than twice that amount—$237 billion—went toward the "tax incentives for individuals" that did virtually nothing to boost the economy. Billions went to help the unemployed, just as in the New Deal, except that in the 1930s the nation got bridges, tunnels, highways, hospitals, schools, libraries, and universities in exchange—because it *employed* the unemployed, instead of just writing them benefit checks. But unemployed people vote, after all; unconceived children do not. We live in a tyranny of the immediate, and costly investments with long returns are a tough sell in an instant-gratification society. Fareed Zakaria calls this the "genetic defect in democracy"—that it "massively overpowers and privileges the present compared to the future."[21]

Even where the political will can be mustered, we often lack the money to make things happen. A public-works campaign on the scale of the New Deal would cost trillions today—money we actually had until recently but chose instead to piss away on desert sands. We fund nation building and infrastructure in Afghanistan and Iraq even as our very own roads, bridges, airports, schools, and hospitals crumble and rust away. What money our states have is increasingly bound up in entitlement programs that are a third-rail issue for politicians seeking elective office. Consider the ill-fated rail link between New York and New Jersey—the ARC Tunnel (Access to the Region's Core). The $9 billion project, already well under way by the fall of 2010, was among the largest public works in the United States. It would have been the first trans-Hudson rail tunnel in a century, adding critically needed capacity to New Jersey Transit's commuter lines, which have seen ridership quadruple since 1984 (trips to Penn Station increased by 150 percent from 2000 to 2010). The tunnel would have created some 6,000 jobs during construction and an estimated 40,000 when completed in 2018. But in October 2010, New Jersey governor Chris Christie canceled the project after rejecting a loan offer from the U.S. Department of Transportation. Christie claimed he did not want to burden New Jersey taxpayers with massive debt. Indeed, the Garden State is already on the verge of bankruptcy, and it's not because of public works. "The New

Jersey state budget," notes Zakaria, "is mostly now devoted to pensions [and] healthcare for state employees."[22] There is simply no money left for building infrastructure, for assuring future competitiveness and economic viability.

One of the most compelling proposals for renewing America's civic infrastructure comes from Vishaan Chakrabarti, one of our most gifted and visionary urbanists. Chakrabarti, who studied city planning at MIT in the early 1990s, served as planning director of the Manhattan office of the New York City Department of City Planning before moving to the real estate sector and becoming the Marc Holliday Professor of Real Estate Development at Columbia University. In a December 2009 essay for the Architectural League of New York's UrbanOmnibus website, Chakrabarti asked readers to imagine the "road not taken" by the Obama administration—one that would have avoided the costly, protracted battle over health care by proposing instead a "silver bullet" reform package aimed at solving several interrelated problems American society currently faces, including the public health crisis. Chakrabarti called it the American Smart Infrastructure Act (ASIA, as if we needed reminding). He asked readers to imagine President Obama saying to the American people:

> We are going to build a new national landscape, and in the process we are going to create jobs, build an innovation economy, rein in health care costs, lower our dependence on foreign oil, and lead the planet to sustainability.
>
> We will build and rebuild infrastructure that lowers greenhouse gas emissions and encourages urban density, emphasizing high-speed rail, transmission grids from alternative energy sources, national internet broadband, and critical roadway maintenance. We will deemphasize all infrastructure that exacerbates emissions, particularly roadway and airport expansion projects. The government will fund approximately $350 billion (about half of TARP) over three years, solving the nation's mobility needs while lowering automobile use and censuring the energy devoured by McMansions. To expedite infrastructure construction and lower costs, NEPA [the National Environmental Policy Act] will be streamlined and project labor agreements will be negotiated with unions. Millions will be employed, pouring liquidity into Main Street.

Health care costs, which are mainly tied to chronic disease stemming from obesity, will lessen as people drive less. As people urbanize in response to new infrastructure and the tax reform described below, rates of diabetes and chronic heart disease will plummet.[23]

How would ASIA be funded? By recouping the $7.8 billion lost each year to traffic congestion; by emissions trading; by phasing out the federal tax deduction for mortgages that has effectively subsidized single-family home ownership for decades now; by imposing a one-dollar-per-gallon gasoline tax. This tax would not only fill federal coffers but also act as a disincentive to driving and better compensate society for the many hidden costs of our automobile culture.

I remember talking about the subject of planning, public works, and national destiny several years ago with a Cambridge, Massachusetts, bartender I had gotten to know when I was teaching at Harvard, a Haitian émigré who had grown up in East New York. He was an infrastructure junkie of sorts and had just returned from visiting his son in Las Vegas; the highlight of his trip was Hoover Dam. I was going on one evening about our crumbling roads and bridges and what they might portend for America's future. After a long pause, my friend shook his head, wiped the bar, and said with a heavy sigh, "Fall of Rome." Bartenders are no fools, and he may well be right. The stakes are so high indeed in this brave new globalizing planet, this world in which American supremacy in all things is no longer a given. It may be wholly unrealistic to expect any single profession, let along one as internally conflicted as ours, to rescue a nation and put it on a green and righteous path. On the other hand, none of the placemaking disciplines are better equipped than ours to help humankind navigate the manifold challenges of a world of cities. Planners alone have the breadth and range of expertise that solving the full spectrum of urban problems and opportunities in the 21st century will require. An extraordinary global urban age is just dawning, and it could well bring about either planning's end or its finest hour. The choice is ours.

# NOTES

## INTRODUCTION: MORE THAN MEETS THE EYE

1. Francis Morrone, "The Triumph of Jane Jacobs," *New York Sun*, September 27, 2007; available at www.nysun.com/arts/triumph-of-jane-jacobs/63089.

2. Jane Jacobs, *The Death and Life of Great American Cities* (New York: Random House, 1961).

3. Jane Jacobs, *The Economy of Cities* (New York: Random House, 1969); and Jane Jacobs, *Cities and the Wealth of Nations* (New York: Random House, 1984). Many years later, while writing an article for *Metropolis* about the International Building Exhibition in Berlin (which ran from 1979 to 1987), I called Jacobs up on the urging of my editor. She picked up the phone and was glad to answer some questions. After making a few observations—"building a suburb in the center of the city is absurd"—she rather quickly declined to comment further: "A person should know the locality, and I haven't been to Berlin." End of conversation.

4. Robert Venturi, *Complexity and Contradiction in Architecture* (New York: Museum of Modern Art and Harry N. Abrams, 1966).

5. Thomas S. Kuhn, *The Structure of Scientific Revolutions* (Chicago: University of Chicago Press, 1962).

6. Walter Benjamin, "Unpacking My Library: A Talk About Book Collecting," in *Illuminations: Essays and Reflections*, ed. Hannah Arendt, trans. Harry Zohn (New York: Schocken, 1969), 59.

7. The filmmaker Ric Burns used most of the final episode in his monumental *New York: A Documentary Film* (PBS, 2003), to tell the story of Jane Jacobs and Robert Moses.

8. Hilary Ballon and Kenneth T. Jackson, eds., *Robert Moses and the Modern City: The Transformation of New York* (New York: W. W. Norton, 2007).

9. Samuel Zipp, *Manhattan Projects: The Rise and Fall of Urban Renewal in Cold War New York* (New York: Oxford University Press, 2010).

10. Jacobs, *Death and Life*.

11. Ibid.

12. Jane Jacobs, *Systems of Survival* (New York: Random House, 1992).

13. Marshall Berman, *All That Is Solid Melts into Air* (New York: Simon and Schuster, 1982), 318.

14. Marshall Berman, "It Happens Every Day," in *The Pragmatist Imagination*, ed. Joan Ockman (New York: Princeton Architectural Press, 2000), excerpted in *Block by Block: Jane Jacobs and the Future of New York*, ed. Timothy Mennel, Jo Steffens, and Christopher Klemek (New York: Municipal Art Society of New York/Princeton Architectural Press, 2007), 49.

15. Carlos Fuentes, "The Mirror of the Other," *Nation*, March 30, 1992, 411.

16. John McPhee, "A Sense of Where You Are," *New Yorker*, January 23, 1965, 42.

17. Jacobs, *Death and Life*, xxiv.

## The Unknown Jane Jacobs: Geographer, Propagandist, City Planning Idealist

1. Jane Jacobs, letter to Chadbourne Gilpatric, July 23, 1959, folder 3381, box 390, series 200R, record group 1.2, Rockefeller Foundation Archives (RFA), Rockefeller Archive Center, Sleepy Hollow, N.Y.

2. *Economic Geography* editors, "News Items: Columbia University, Department of Geography," *Economic Geography* 2 (April 1926): 332.

3. Harlan H. Barrows, "Geography as Human Ecology," *Annals of the Association of American Geographers* 13 (March 1923): 1, 3.

4. Jane Jacobs, *Cities and the Wealth of Nations: Principles of Economic Life* (New York: Random House, 1984), 110–23.

5. Jane Jacobs, *Dark Age Ahead* (New York: Random House, 2004), 177–78.

6. Jacobs also cited Pirenne's *Early Democracies in the Low Countries* (New York: Harper & Row, 1963) in *Systems of Survival* (New York: Random House, 1992).

7. Jane Jacobs, interview by Chadbourne Gilpatric, June 4, 1958, folder 3380, box 390, series 200R, record group 1.2, RFA.

8. Jane Jacobs, *The Death and Life of Great American Cities* (1961; New York: Modern Library, 1993), xvi.

9. Jane Butzner [Jacobs], "Caution, Men Working," *Cue, the Weekly Magazine of New York Life*, May 18, 1940, 24.

10. Jane Jacobs, *Systems of Survival* (New York: Random House, 1992), xi.

11. Ibid., 20.

12. Jane Jacobs, letter to Ms. Talmey, November 22, 1961, Jane Jacobs Papers, MS95-29, box 13, folder 12, John J. Burns Library, Boston College, Chestnut Hill, Mass. A slightly different version of the autobiographical account in this letter is republished in Max Allen's *Ideas That Matter: The Worlds of Jane Jacobs* (Owen Sound, Ontario: Ginger Press, 1997), 3. The change gives a sense of Jacobs's attention to her own narrative.

13. "Jane Butzner Jacobs," July 20, 1948, file no. 123-252, FBI, New York, 4–5.

14. Jane Butzner [Jacobs], "Trylon's Steel Helps to Build Big New Nickel Plant in Cuba," *New York Herald Tribune*, December 27, 1942.

15. Jane Butzner [Jacobs], "Women Wanted to Fill 2,795 Kinds of Jobs," *New York Herald Tribune*, October 18, 1942.

16. Jane Butzner [Jacobs], "WAVES and WAACs Go Through the Assignment Classification Mill," *New York Herald Tribune*, March 28, 1943.

17. "30,000 Unemployed and 7,000 Empty Houses in Scranton, Neglected City," *Iron Age* 151 (March 25, 1943), 94.

18. The story of Jacobs's Scranton campaign is nicely told in Glenna Lang and Marjory Wunsch's *Genius of Common Sense: Jane Jacobs and the Story of The Death and Life of Great American Cities* (Boston: David R. Godine, 2009), 31–32, 115. They reproduce the letter from the chamber of commerce's representative, E. M. Elliott, to the editors of *Iron Age*, April 17, 1943, in their well-written book.

19. Jacobs, *Systems of Survival*, 215.

20. Office of War Information, "Justification for Rapid Promotion" for Jane Butzner [Jacobs], October 3, 1944, National Personnel Records Center, St. Louis.

21. Howard Oiseth, "The First Magazine," in *The Way It Was: USIA's Press and Publications Service (1935–77)* (Washington, D.C.: U.S. Information Agency, 1977), 57. I am indebted to Martin Manning of the State Department for this article and related histories of State Department and USIA publications.

22. Creighton Peet, "Russian 'Amerika,' A Magazine about U.S. for Soviet Citizens," *College Art Journal*, Fall 1951, 18.

23. Oiseth, "First Magazine," 57.

24. Jane Jacobs, Application for Federal Employment, September 8, 1949, Attachment A, 6, National Personnel Records Center, St. Louis.

25. "Rosenfield and His Hospitals: He Approaches His Jobs Like a City Planner," *Architectural Forum* 97 (September 1952), 128.

26. "New Thinking on Shopping Centers," *Architectural Forum* 98 (March 1953), 122.

27. Ibid.

28. Jane Jacobs, "Washington: 20th Century Capital?" *Architectural Forum* 104 (January 1956), 92–115.

29. "Typical Downtown Transformed: The Fort Worth Plan," *Architectural Forum* 104 (May 1956), 147.

30. "Philadelphia's Redevelopment: A Progress Report," *Architectural Forum* 103 (July 1955), 120.

31. Ed Bacon, quoted in "Urban Design: Condensed Report of an Invitation Conference, Harvard University, April 9–10, 1956," *Progressive Architecture* 37 (August 1956), 108.

32. "Philadelphia's Redevelopment," 118.

33. Jacobs, *Death and Life*, 448.

34. Lewis Mumford, "Mother Jacobs' Home Remedies," *New Yorker*, December 1, 1962, 148–79.

35. Jane Jacobs to Mayor Robert F. Wagner and Borough President Hulan Jack, June 1, 1955, Shirley Hayes Papers, box 3, folder 10, The New-York Historical Society.

36. Ellen Lurie, "East Harlem Small Business Survey & Planning Committee Fact Sheet," January 16, 1956, folder 7, box 35, series V, Union Settlement Association Records (USAR), Union Settlement Association Papers, Rare Book and Manuscript Library, Columbia University, New York, 1. Some of the figures quoted in the fact sheet were already quoted in "Shops a Problem in East Harlem," *New York Times*, May 8, 1955.

37. Ellen Lurie, draft of essay for *Architectural Forum*, "The Dreary Deadlock of Public Housing," folder 7, box 35, series V, USAR, 1. Jacobs edited Lurie's essay for the "Dreary Deadlock" feature and took this language out, apparently in order to expand awareness of the problems of public housing and urban renewal beyond the limits of East Harlem.

38. Jane Jacobs, letter to Grady Clay, March 3, 1959, Personal Papers of Grady Clay; copy supplied by Clay. I am indebted to Grady Clay and Judith McCandless for their kindness and assistance with this research.

39. Jacobs, letter to Chadbourne Gilpatric, July 23, 1959.

## An Australian Jane Jacobs

1. Jane Jacobs, *The Death and Life of Great American Cities* (New York: Random House, 1961).

2. Blair Badcock, *Unfairly Structured Cities* (Oxford: Basil Blackwell, 1984).

3. Hugh Stretton, *Ideas for Australian Cities* (Adelaide, Australia: Hugh Stretton, 1970), 217.

4. Ibid.

5. Margo Huxley, personal communication, October 22, 2010.

6. Leonie Sandercock, personal communication, November 14, 2010.

7. Robert Freestone, "The Americanization of Australian Planning," *Journal of Planning History* 3, no. 3 (2004): 187–214.

8. Tony Powell, "The 1960s: Planning for Growth and Change," in *Sydney: Planning or Politics, Town Planning for Sydney Region since 1945*, ed J. Toon and J. Falk (Sydney, Australia: Planning Research Centre, University of Sydney, 2003), 86.

9. Leonie Sandercock, "Educating Planners: From Physical Determinism to Economic Crisis," in *Urban Political Economy: The Australian Case*, ed. L. Sandercock and M. Berry (Sydney, Australia: George Allen and Unwin, 1983), 38.

10. Robert Freestone, personal communication, November 25, 2010.

11. Robert J. Payne, "Public Participation in the Urban Planning Process," *Royal Australian Planning Institute Journal* 11 (1973): 29

12. See David Harvey, *Social Justice and the City* (Baltimore: Johns Hopkins University Press, 1973).

13. Leslie Kilmartin, David Thorns, and Terry Burke, *Social Theory and the Australian City* (Sydney, Australia: George Allen and Unwin, 1985), 66.

14. Margo Huxley, personal communication, November 14, 2010. For an elaboration of the problem of Jacobs for Marxist-inspired scholars, see Hugh Stretton, *Urban Planning in Rich and Poor Countries* (Oxford: Oxford University Press, 1978).

15. Badcock, *Unfairly Structured Cities*, 143–44.

16. Stretton, *Ideas for Australian Cities*, 216–17.

17. Pat Troy, personal communication, November 7, 2010.

18. Lewis Mumford, *The City in History: Its Origins, Its Transformations, and Its Prospects* (New York: Harcourt, Brace, and World, 1961).

19. Sandercock, personal communication.

20. Stretton, *Ideas for Australian Cities*, 216.

21. Ibid., 217.

22. Sandercock, personal communication.

23. I would like to thank the following colleagues for discussing ideas, sharing anecdotes, and allowing me to quote their views: Stephen Cairns, Ruth Fincher, Patsy Healey, Michael Hebbert, Lionel Orchard, Bill Randolph, Kate Shaw, Patricia Stretton, and Suzanne Tonkin. And special thanks to Robert Freestone, Margo Huxley, Leonie Sandercock, and Pat Troy: Margo for her reflections and for pulling out quotable quotes from her personal—but conveniently for me, U.K.-based—library on Australian urban planning; Robert, Leonie, and Pat for their candid and fulsome reflections.

## THE LITERARY CRAFT OF JANE JACOBS

1. Jane Jacobs to Chadbourne Gilpatric, July 17, 1959, folder 3381, box 390, series 200R, record group 1.2, Rockefeller Foundation Archives (RFA), Rockefeller Archive Center, Sleepy Hollow, N.Y.

2. Jane Jacobs to Chadbourne Gilpatric, March 17, 1960, folder 3381, box 390, series 200R, record group 1.2, RFA.

3. Jane Jacobs, interview by Leticia Kent, "More Babies Needed, Not Fewer," *Vogue* 156 (August 15, 1970): 86.

4. Adele Freedman, "Jane Jacobs," *Globe and Mail* (Toronto), June 9, 1984.

5. See Leslie Katz, "Voice in the Wilderness," *Nation*, March 3, 1962, 198–99; Wolf Von Eckardt, "Urban Planning Stirs a Storm," *Washington Post*, December 29, 1962; Howard Husock, "Urban Iconoclast: Jane Jacobs Revisited," *City Journal*, Winter 1994; Mark Feeney, "City Sage," *Boston Globe*, November 14, 1993; Robert Fulford, "Abattoir for Sacred Cows: Three Decades in the Life of a Classic," in *Ideas That Matter: The Worlds of Jane Jacobs*, ed. Max Allen (Owen Sound, Ontario: Ginger Press, 1997), 5–10; and Peter Dreier, "Jane Jacobs's Legacy," *City & Community* 5 (2006): 227–31.

6. See Christopher Klemek, "From Political Outsider to Power Broker in Two 'Great American Cities': Jane Jacobs and the Fall of the Urban Renewal Order in New York and Toronto," *Journal of Urban History* 34 (January 2008): 309–32; and Peter Laurence, "The Death and Life of Urban Design: Jane Jacobs, The Rockefeller Foundation and the New Research in Urbanism, 1955–65," *Journal of Urban Design* 11 (June 2006): 145–72.

7. Jane Jacobs to Chadbourne Gilpatric, July 1, 1958, folder 3380, box 390, series 200R, record group 1.2, RFA.

8. Jacobs, for instance, praised the City Planning Commission's West Side Urban Renewal study as the "first small portent" of an alternative to the "ruthless, raw-material approach to New York" that had been destroying the city's "economic and social relationships just as swiftly and efficiently as rebuilding money can destroy them." Jane Jacobs, untitled manuscript, April 20, 1958, Jane Jacobs Papers, MS95-29, folder 8, box 25, Burns Library, Boston College, Chestnut Hill, Mass., 8, 3.

9. Jane Jacobs to Chadbourne Gilpatric, June 14, 1958, folder 3380, box 390, series 200R, record group 1.2, RFA.

10. Catherine Bauer to Chadbourne Gilpatric, August 5, 1958, folder 3380, box 390, series 200R, record group 1.2, RFA.

11. See Charles Dickens, *Sketches by "Boz," Illustrative of Every-Day Life, and Every-Day People* (London: John Macrone, 1836); and George G. Foster, *New York by Gas-Light: With Here and There a Streak of Sunshine*, ed. Stuart M. Blumin (1856; Berkeley: University of California Press, 1990).

12. Jane Butzner [Jacobs], "Flowers Come to Town," *Vogue* 89 (February 15, 1937): 113.

13. Jane Jacobs, *The Death and Life of Great American Cities* (New York: Random House, 1961), 4.

14. For an account of some of the writers who explored the second ghetto during this period, see Carlo Rotella, *October Cities: The Redevelopment of Urban Literature* (Berkeley: University of California Press, 1998).

15. Jacobs, *Death and Life*, 44.

16. Ibid., 40.

17. Ibid., 112.

18. For a thorough and culturally attentive history of the hard-boiled genre, see Sean McCann, *Gumshoe America: Hard-Boiled Crime Fiction and the Rise and Fall of New Deal Liberalism* (Durham, N.C.: Duke University Press, 2000); and Leonard Cassuto, *Hard-Boiled Sentimentality: The Secret History of American Crime Stories* (New York: Columbia University Press, 2009).

19. Jacobs, *Death and Life*, 314, 4.

20. Ibid., 5.

21.  Gilpatric, in fact, informed Jacobs that there was "too much quotation of and reference to Kevin Lynch" after he had read a draft of *Death and Life*. Chadbourne Gilpatric to Jane Jacobs, March 27, 1961, folder 3381, box 390, series 200R, record group 1.2, RFA.

22.  Kevin Lynch, *The Image of the City* (Cambridge, Mass.: MIT Press, 1960), 4, 3.

23.  Jacobs, *Death and Life*, 14, 51, 134, 265, 325.

24.  Ibid., 15, 4.

25.  Ibid., 4.

26.  Ibid., 8, 25, 34, 46, 90.

27.  See Jane Jacobs, "The Missing Link in City Redevelopment," *Architectural Forum* 104 (June 1956): 132–33.

28.  Jane Jacobs, "Reason, Emotion, Pressure: There Is No Other Recipe," *Village Voice*, May 22, 1957, 4.

29.  Jacobs, *Death and Life*, 13.

30.  Ibid., 9, 56.

31.  Charles Abrams et al., "Abattoir for Sacred Cows," *Progressive Architecture*, April 1962, 196.

32.  Jacobs to Gilpatric, July 17, 1959.

33.  Jane Jacobs to Chadbourne Gilpatric, July 23, 1959, folder 3381, box 390, series 200R, record group 1.2, RFA.

34.  Jane Jacobs, *The Nature of Economies* (New York: Random House, 2000), x.

35.  Dennis O'Harrow, "Jacobin Revival," in *Ideas That Matter: The Worlds of Jane Jacobs*, ed. Max Allen (Owen Sound, Ontario: Ginger Press, 1997), 9–10. Originally published in *American Society of Planning Officials Newsletter*, February 1962.

## Urban Warfare: The Battles for Buenos Aires

1.  This information was gathered in a series of long conversations with San Telmo residents during the weeks of the conflict in mid-2009.

2.  Both books were translated by Angel Abad for Ediciones Península. *The Death and Life of Great American Cities* was published as *Muerte y vida de las grandes ciudades*. *The Economy of Cities* was issued as *La economía de las ciudades* and was never reprinted.

3.  At the Taller 4 at Universidad Nacional de Córdoba, by Professor Julio Borges; the Escuela Técnica Superior de Arquitectura de Madrid; and the Escola de Arquitetura da Universidades Federal de Santa Catarina. This list is incomplete but gives an idea of the geographical scope involved.

4.  Those blogs, and many others, reproduced a story by the Spanish national daily *El País* (Madrid), on Jacobs's death. *El Malpensante*, originating in Colombia, published a fictional interview with her, in which her "answers" had been collated from her writings and other interviews.

5.  See, for example, *Santiago Pusso v. City of Buenos Aires*, over the building permit for a 23-story building in Northern Barracas, a low-rise area, filed in March 2010 in Buenos Aires.

6.  It was Basta de Demoler's second legal challenge to the demolition of a historic landmark. In the first challenge, the NGO found out, to its chagrin, that private property rights trumped all their cultural, community, and historical arguments. For the second challenge they were advised by city councilwoman Teresa de Anchorena; her senior adviser, Facundo de Almeida; and a lawyer volunteering his time, Diego Hickethier. The issue turned into nothing less than a constitutional matter, with Basta de Demoler arguing that if the executive branch authorized the destruction of a building being considered for landmarking by the legislature, it effectively prevented the legislative branch from acting. The finding of the court was not only upheld on appeal but extended to all similar cases.

7.  A few days later, a mezzanine collapsed at a popular dance club in Palermo Viejo, Buenos Aires, hurting several revelers. There was no indication that the place had ever been inspected by the city or that anybody had ever asked for a license to build the mezzanine.

8.  Buenos Aires, a federal territory until 1999, is now a state in the union.

## THE MAGPIE AND THE BEE:
## JANE JACOBS'S MAGNIFICENT OBSESSION

1.  E. H. Carr, *What Is History?* (London: Macmillan, 1961), 23.

2.  The works by Jane Jacobs I refer to in this essay are *The Death and Life of Great American Cities* (1961; New York: Modern Library, 1993); *The Economy of Cities* (New York: Random House, 1969); and *Cities and the Wealth of Nations* (New York: Random House, 1984).

3.  Its two relevant predecessors were the Social Science Citation Index and the Arts and Humanities Citation Index. The online versions of those databases are available from 1975. In dissecting these databases, the able assistance of Amy Skippen is gratefully acknowledged. In Figure 1, counts are reported for pairs of years to help smooth random variations.

4.  Herbert Gans, "Urban Vitality and the Fallacy of Physical Determinism," in *People and Plans: Essays on Urban Problems and Solutions* (New York: Basic Books, 1968), 30–40 (essay originally published in *Commentary*, February 1962); Lewis Mumford, "Mother Jacobs' Home Remedies," *New Yorker*, December 1, 1962, 148–79. For typically sympathetic discussion of criticism of Jacobs, see Alice S. Alexiou, *Jane Jacobs: Urban Visionary* (New Brunswick, N.J.: Rutgers University Press, 2006), 82–94, 135–36; Anthony Cichello, "In Defense of Jane Jacobs: An Appreciative Overview," in *Ethics in Making a Living: The Jane Jacobs Conference*, ed. Fred Lawrence (Atlanta: Scholars Press, 1989), 115–41. Gans's later assessment suggests that her own experience had led Jacobs to romanticize the city: Herbert Gans, "Jane Jacobs: Towards an Understanding of *The Death and Life of Great American Cities*," *City and Community* 5, no. 3 (2006): 213–15. This is consistent with Benjamin Schwarz's commentary in "Gentrification and Its Dis-

contents: Manhattan Never Was What We Think It Was," *Atlantic*, June 2010, 85–89. The long-term increase in the number of urban citations is due to at least two factors: The Web of Science database has steadily expanded the number of journals included in its database, while several leading journals—for example, *Urban Studies*—now publish more frequently.

5. Roger Montgomery, "Is There Still Life in 'The Death and Life'?" *Journal of the American Planning Association* 64, no. 3 (1998): 271. The best concise summary of *Death and Life* is in David R. Hill, "Jane Jacobs' Ideas on Big, Diverse Cities," *Journal of the American Planning Association* 54, no. 3 (1988): 302–14.

6. The best concise outline of Jacobs's arguments about the urban economy is in Pierre Desrochers and Gert-Jan Hospers, "Cities and the Economic Development of Nations: An Essay on Jane Jacobs' Contribution to Economic Theory," *Canadian Journal of Regional Science* 30, no. 1 (2007): 115–30.

7. *Handbook of Regional and Urban Economics*, eds. H. Vernon Henderson and Jacques François-Thisse, vol. 4, *Cities and Geography* (Amsterdam: Elsevier, 2004).

8. Timothy Mennel, Jo Steffens, and Christopher Klemek, eds., *Block by Block: Jane Jacobs and the Future of New York* (New York: Princeton Architectural Press, 2007).

9. This analysis was undertaken on July 15, 2010. Later tabulations will vary somewhat, of course.

10. Two of the four are review articles, while the other two are by the geographer Peter Taylor and the urbanist Richard Florida, writers who have been unusually active in rearticulating and testing Jacobs's ideas: Richard Florida and C. Mellender, "There Goes the Metro: How and Why Bohemians, Artists and Gays Affect Regional Housing Values," *Journal of Economic Geography* 10, no. 2 (2010): 167–88; Peter Taylor, "Problematizing City/State Relations: Towards a Geohistorical Understanding of Contemporary Globalization," *Transactions, Institute of British Geographers* 32, no. 2 (2007): 133–50. See also Richard Florida, *The Rise of the Creative Class* (New York: Basic Books, 2002); Richard Florida, *Cities and the Creative Class* (London: Routledge, 2005); and Peter J. Taylor, "Jane Jacobs (1916–2006): An Appreciation," *Environment and Planning A* 38 (2006): 1,981–92. Taylor is leading a research project exploring Jacobs's ideas about cities and economic growth in world history. Preliminary results are reported in Peter J. Taylor, A. Firth, A. M. Hoyler, and D. Smith, "Explosive City Growth in the Modern World-System: An Initial Inventory Derived from Urban Demographic Changes," *Urban Geography* 31 (2010): 865–84. For an overview, see www.lboro.ac.uk/gawc/projects/projec55.html. Also active in testing Jacobs's ideas is Edward Glaeser. See Edward L. Glaeser, Hedi D. Kallal, Jose A. Schinkman, and Andrei Shleifer, "Growth in Cities," *Journal of Political Economy* 100, no. 6 (1992): 1,126–52; Edward L. Glaeser, "Cities and Ethics: An Essay for Jane Jacobs," *Journal of Urban Affairs* 22, no. 4 (2000): 473–93.

11. Peter Laurence, "Jane Jacobs Before *Death and Life*," *Journal of the Society of Architectural Historians* 66, no. 1 (2007): 12; Desrochers and Hospers, "Cities and Economic Development," 118, 125; Jacobs, *Economy of Cities*, 3; Florida, *Rise of the Creative Class*, 222.

12. Richard C. Keeley, "Some Paths Through Jane Jacobs's Thought," in Lawrence, *Ethics in Making a Living*, 34–35; Jacobs, *Death and Life*, 65–71. Jacobs also wrote at length about how the complexity of cities requires an appropriately complex, flexible, and inductive methodology. See Jacobs, *Death and Life*, 558–85.

13. I would speculate that the reason why Jacobs's approach in *Cities and Wealth* is exceptional is that she was especially anxious to be taken seriously on this subject. This is consistent with her comment, made late in life in the course of a private interview, that she believed her main intellectual contribution had been to economic theory. Jane Jacobs, interview by Pierre Desrochers, Sanford Ikeda, Gert-Jan Hospers, and Hiroko Shimizu, Toronto, March 15, 2004, transcript provided by Pierre Desrochers and used with permission, henceforth referred to as "Jacobs, interview, 2004."

14. Joseph Schumpeter, "Science and Ideology," *American Economic Review* 39 (March 1949): 351, 359; Carr, *What Is History?*, 29.

15. Keeley, "Some Paths Through Jane Jacobs's Thought," 35.

16. Charles Tilly, "How I Work," *Evolutionary Theories in the Social Sciences* (originally published 2002); available at http://etss.net/evolution/how_i_work/tilly.htm.

17. Mumford, "Mother Jacobs' Home Remedies," 158.

18. Montgomery's comments were made in the course of a plenary presentation at the biennial meetings of the Society for American City and Regional Planning History in Seattle. I am indebted to the recollections of Eric Sandweiss, personal communications, November 8, 2007, and August 17, 2010.

19. Jacobs, *Cities and Wealth*, 48; Ronald Dore, *Shinohata: A Portrait of a Japanese Village* (New York: Pantheon, 1978); Ronald Dore, personal communication, August 18, 2010.

20. In a delightful and apparently unintended irony, *Beneath the Bull Ring*, Simon Buteux's recent account of archaeological work at a renewed Bull Ring, is subtitled *The Archaeology of Life and Death in Early Birmingham* (Studley, Warwickshire, U.K.: Brewin Books, 2003). On Henry's, see http://birminghammusicarchive.co.uk/?page_id=779.

21. Asa Briggs, *Victorian Cities* (1963; Berkeley and Los Angeles: University of California Press, 1993); Jacobs, *The Economy of Cities*.

22. Gordon Cherry, *Birmingham: A Study in Geography, History and Planning* (Chichester, West Sussex, U.K.: John Wiley and Sons, 1994), 81. Briggs uses the quote from *Harper's* for a chapter title in his *History of Birmingham*, vol. 2, *1865–1938* (London: Oxford University Press, 1952).

23. Steven Johnson, *Where Good Ideas Come From: The Natural History of Innovation* (New York: Riverhead, 2010), 16–21, 160–62, 199–200.

24. Peter Hall, "Creative Cities and Economic Development," *Urban Studies* 37, no. 4 (2000): 642; Gans, "Jane Jacobs," 213; Herbert Gans, personal communication, September 19, 2010; Montgomery, "Is There Still Life," 271; Alexiou, *Jane Jacobs*, 197.

25. Marc Van der Mieroop, *The Ancient Mesopotamian City* (Oxford: Oxford University Press, 1997), 25; Michael Smith, "V. Gordon Childe and the Urban Revolution: An Historical Perspective on a Revolution in Urban Studies," *Town Planning Review* 80 (2009): 7n2; Michael Smith, personal communication, October 25, 2008. For a recent defense of Jacobs's arguments about the urban origins of agriculture, see Peter Taylor, "Extraordinary Cities I: Early 'City-ness' and the Invention of Agriculture," *GaWC Research Bulletin No. 359*; available at www.lboro.ac.uk/gawc/rb/rb359.html; Jacobs, interview, 2004.

26. Alexiou, *Jane Jacobs*, 174.

27. Hill, "Jane Jacobs' Ideas," 309. Richard White has argued that after she moved to Toronto, Jacobs "unfailingly directed her own energy into writing rather than protesting." Richard White, "Jane Jacobs and the Transformation of Toronto Planning, 1968–1978," *Journal of Planning History* (forthcoming). Note that those who have drawn most broadly on Jacobs's ideas have not shown the same neglect of municipal government. In Toronto, for example, under Richard Florida's direction, the Martin Prosperity Institute made strategic interventions in the mayoral campaign in the fall of 2010. See, for example, Karen King, Brian Hracs, Mark Denstedt, and Kevin Stolarick, "The Importance of Diversity to the Economic and Social Prosperity of Toronto" (long paper, Martin Prosperity Institute, August 2010), available at http://martinprosperity.org/media/pdfs/Toronto_election_series-Importance_of_Diversity_to_Economic_and_Social_Prosperity.pdf.

28. Hill, "Jane Jacobs' Ideas," 306–7, 311; Gans, "Urban Vitality"; Jacobs, interview, 2004. On Jacobs's use of fractals, see Sanford Ikeda, "Jane Jacobs," *The Freeman: Ideas on Liberty*; available at www.thefreemanonline.org/featured/jane-jacobs/#.

29. I would like to thank Amy Skippen for assistance, together with Ronald Dore, Christopher Klemek, Peter Laurence, Eric Sandweiss, and especially Pierre Desrochers and Sanford Ikeda for sharing information. Pierre Desrochers, Richard Florida, Herbert Gans, Sanford Ikeda, Peter Laurence, Timothy Mennel, Robert Morris, Max Page, Eric Sandweiss, Michael Smith, Peter Taylor, Carol Town, and Richard White made valuable comments on an earlier draft. The Arts Research Board at McMaster University provided financial assistance.

## JANE JACOBS IN DUTCH CITIES AND TOWNS: METROPOLITAN ROMANCE IN PROVINCIAL REALITY

1. See Jeroen den Uyl, "IJburg is 'Jane Jacobs-proof'!"; available at www.mediamatic.net/page/108488/en.

2. See the 12 contributions by Dutch authors, planners, and policy makers in S. Franke and G. J. Hospers, eds., *De Levende Stad: Over de Hedendaagse Betekenis van Jane Jacobs* (Amsterdam: SUN/Trancity, 2009).

3. C. Klemek, "Placing Jane Jacobs within the Transatlantic Urban Conversation," *Journal of the American Planning Association* 73, no. 1 (2007): 49–67.

4.  I. de Wolfe, "The Death and Life of Great American Citizens," *Architectural Review* 133 (1963): 91.

5.  M. Allen, *Ideas That Matter: The Worlds of Jane Jacobs* (Toronto: Ginger Press, 1997), 87.

6.  J. Gehl, *Life Between Buildings: Using Public Space* (Copenhagen: Danish Architectural Press, 1987).

7.  A. J. van Duren, *De Dynamiek van de Constante: Over de Flexibiliteit van de Amsterdamse Binnenstad als Economische Plaats* (Utrecht: Jan van Arkel, 1995).

8.  J. Jacobs, interview by S. Brand, "Vital Cities," *Whole Earth*, Winter 1998, 1–4; A. Tobin, "Urban Planning Guru Jane Jacobs on the Traps We Set for Ourselves," *Canadian Press* 27 (March 2000): 1–3; G. J. Hospers, "Jane Jacobs: Her Life and Work," *European Planning Studies* 14 (2006): 723–32.

9.  J. Jacobs, *Cities and the Wealth of Nations* (New York: Random House, 1984).

10. J. Jacobs, *Systems of Survival: A Dialogue on the Moral Foundations of Commerce and Politics* (New York: Random House, 1992).

11. J. Jacobs, *The Death and Life of Great American Cities* (New York: Random House, 1961), 189.

12. See, for example, J. Saris, S. van Dommelen, and T. Metze, eds., *Nieuwe Ideeën voor Oude Gebouwen: Creatieve Economie en Stedelijke Herontwikkeling* (Rotterdam: NAi Uitgevers, 2008).

13. T. Blokland, *Oog voor Elkaar: Veiligheidsbeleving en Sociale Controle in de Grote Stad* (Amsterdam: Amsterdam University Press, 2009).

14. M. van Twist, W. J. Verheul, and M. van der Steen, *Ondernemerschap en Grensverleggende Praktijken* (The Hague: In Axis, 2008).

15. Van Duren, *De Dynamiek van de Constante*.

16. G4 and G27, *Toekomst Stedelijk Economisch Beleid: Bidbook G4 en G27* (Amersfoort, Netherlands: BMC, 2009).

17. O. ten Wolde, "De bedrijvigheid terug in de buurt," *Talis Trends*, June 2008, 1–5.

18. B. Colenbrander and A. Lengkeek, *Op Locatie: Enschede na de Vuurwerkramp* (Rotterdam: Uitgeverij 010, 2008).

19. Ibid.

20. Jacobs, *Death and Life*, 120–21.

21. W. van Aggelen and N. Kleene, *Kijk op de Wijk: Kansarm of Kansrijk?* (Amsterdam: ABN AMRO Economisch Bureau, 2008).

22. Ten Wolde, "De bedrijvigheid terug in de buurt."

23. S. Zukin, *Naked City: The Death and Life of Authentic Urban Places* (New York: Oxford University Press, 2010).

24. Jacobs, *Death and Life*, vii.

25. J. Jacobs, "Where to Locate a Bookstore in a City and Where Not to Locate One," *Publishers Weekly*, January 1962, 28–31.

26. J. Jacobs, interview by B. Harris, "Cities and Web Economies," *Government Technology* (2002), 3; available at www.newcolonist.com/jane_jacobs.html.

## TIME, SCALE, AND CONTROL: HOW NEW URBANISM (MIS)USES JANE JACOBS

1. J. Grant, *Planning the Good Community: New Urbanism in Theory and Practice* (London: Routledge, 2006).

2. "New Urbanism," Wikipedia; available at http://en.wikipedia.org/wiki/New_Urbanism. See also J. Kunstler, "Interview with Jane Jacobs" (September 6, 2000, for *Metropolis Magazine*, March 2001); available at www.kunstler.com/mags_jacobs1.htm.

3. J. Jacobs, *The Death and Life of Great American Cities* (New York: Random House, 1961).

4. Ibid., 96.

5. H. J. Gans, *The Levittowners: Ways of Life and Politics in a New Suburban Community* (New York: Pantheon, 1967); H. J. Gans, *The Urban Villagers: Group and Class in the Life of Italian-Americans* (New York: Free Press of Glencoe, 1962); H. J. Gans, *People and Plans: Essays on Urban Problems and Solutions* (New York: Penguin Books, 1968).

6. A. Duany, E. Plater-Zyberk, and J. Speck, *Suburban Nation: The Rise of Sprawl and the Decline of the American Dream* (New York: North Point Press, 2000) 60.

7. For instance, while planners in Toronto found Jacobs compelling and began to apply her principles in the 1970s, as late as the 1980s planners in smaller cities such as Halifax, Nova Scotia, were openly critical of Jacobs's naïveté. See J. Sewell, *The Shape of the City: Toronto Struggles with Modern Planning* (Toronto: University of Toronto Press, 1993); J. Grant, *The Drama of Democracy: Contention and Dispute in Community Planning* (Toronto: University of Toronto Press, 1994), 129–30.

8. Sewell, *Shape of the City.*

9. Grant, *Planning the Good Community*, 153–56. J. Vischer, "Community and Privacy: Planners' Intentions and Residents' Reactions," *Plan Canada* 23, no. 4 (1984): 112–22.

10. For instance, early writings by Peter Calthorpe and discussions of Duany's early projects do not cite Jacobs as a source. See P. Calthorpe, *The Next American Metropolis* (New York: Princeton Architectural Press, 1993). A. Krieger, *Andres Duany and Elizabeth Plater-Zyberk: Towns and Town-Making Principles* (Cambridge, Mass.: Harvard University Graduate School of Design, 1991).

11. J. Adler, "The New Burb Is a Village," *Newsweek* 124, no. 26 (December 26, 1994/January 2, 1995): 109.

12. D. Mohney and K. Easterling, *Seaside: Making a Town in America* (New York: Princeton Architectural Press, 1991).

13. A. Duany and E. Plater-Zyberk, "The Second Coming of the American Small Town," *Wilson Quarterly* 16, no. 1 (1992): 19–48; Krieger, *Andres Duany and Elizabeth Plater-Zyberk*.

14. Salingaros calls Krier the "intellectual godfather of the New Urbanism movement": N. Salingaros, "The Future of Cities: The Absurdity of Modernism," *Planetizen*; available at www.planetizen.com/oped/item.php?id=35. Scully points to Krier's influence on Duany and Plater-Zyberk: V. Scully, "Seaside and New Haven," in Krieger, *Andres Duany and Elizabeth Plater-Zyberk*, 17–20. Salingaros quotes Duany indicating that Krier inspired him to create traditional communities: N. Salingaros, "Léon Krier: Architect and Urban Planner"; available at http://zakuski.math.utsa.edu/krier.

15. M. Leccese and K. McCormick, *Charter of the New Urbanism* (New York: McGraw-Hill, 2000). See also N. Calavita, "The New Urbanism," *Journal of the American Planning Association* 60, no. 4 (1994): 534; P. Katz, *The New Urbanism: Toward an Architecture of Community* (New York: McGraw-Hill, 1994).

16. See, for example, R. Ewing, *Best Development Practices: Doing the Right Thing and Making Money at the Same Time* (Chicago: APA Planners Press, 1996); E. Talen, *New Urbanism and American Planning: The Conflict of Cultures* (New York: Routledge, 2005).

17. Jacobs, *Death and Life*, 183; Krieger, *Andres Duany and Elizabeth Plater-Zyberk*, 70; Duany, Plater-Zyberk, and Speck, *Suburban Nation*, 88.

18. Jacobs, *Death and Life*, 150–51.

19. E. Talen, "Design That Enables Diversity: The Complications of a Planning Ideal," *Journal of Planning Literature* 20, no. 3 (2006): 233–49; Talen, *Design for Diversity: Exploring Socially Mixed Neighborhoods* (Oxford: Architectural Press, 2008).

20. For instance, see A. Marshall, *How Cities Work: Suburbs, Sprawl, and the Road Not Taken* (Austin: University of Texas Press, 2000).

21. E. Talen, "The Unbearable Lightness of New Urbanism," in *New Urbanism and Beyond: Designing Cities for the Future*, ed. T. Haas (New York: Rizzoli, 2008), 77.

22. As early as 1994, evaluations of new urbanism practices identified challenges it had meeting its social agenda. See I. A. Audirac and A. H. Shermyen, "An Evaluation of Neotraditional Design's Social Prescription: Postmodern Placebo or Remedy for Suburban Malaise?" *Journal of Planning Education and Research* 13, no. 3 (1994): 161–73.

23. The index of Talen's book on new urbanism and American planning lists 61 page references where she highlights Jacobs's work and influence. See Talen, *New Urbanism and American Planning*, 313.

24. Talen, *Design for Diversity*, 7.

25. Talen, "Design That Enables Diversity," 234.

26. Ibid., 342.

27. Jacobs, *Death and Life*, 150.

28. Ibid., 187.

29. Ibid., 138–39.

30. Ibid., 190–91.

31. Codes in new urbanism projects set out the requirements for corner stores. See K. Anderson, "Oldfangled New Towns," *Time* 137 (May 20, 1991): 52–55. See also "15 Ways to Fix the Suburbs," *Newsweek* 125, no. 20 (May 15, 1995): 46–53.

32. Duany, Plater-Zyberk, and Speck, *Suburban Nation*, 190.

33. Katz, *New Urbanism*, x.

34. Anderson, "Oldfangled New Towns," 52.

35. Krieger, *Andres Duany and Elizabeth Plater-Zyberk*, 15.

36. Duany and Plater-Zyberk, "Second Coming."

37. Jacobs, *Death and Life*, 114.

38. Ibid., 119. Jacobs saw 30,000 residents as sufficient to constitute a functional district in cities the size of Boston, but suggested a functional district might need to include 80,000 or more in larger cities such as New York: ibid., 130–31.

39. Ibid., 145–46.

40. While the Charter of the New Urbanism advocates planning at all scales from the region down to the neighborhood, in practice most development projects occur at a smaller scale. See "Charter of the New Urbanism," *Congress for the New Urbanism*; available at www.cnu.org/charter.

41. Adler, "The New Burb Is a Village"; Krieger, *Andres Duany and Elizabeth Plater-Zyberk*.

42. Duany, Plater-Zyberk, and Speck, *Suburban Nation*, 148, 191–92.

43. Kunstler, "Interview with Jane Jacobs." McInnes includes a similar comment from Jacobs: "Instead of aiming at big projects, it's much better to aim at the small ones, like infill projects." C. McInnes, "Toronto Planners Praised by Jacobs," *Globe and Mail* (Toronto), September 7, 1991, Metro edition, A4.

44. Jacobs, *Death and Life*, 122–29.

45. Duany, Plater-Zyberk, and Speck, *Suburban Nation*, 42, 194.

46. J. Jacobs, *Cities and the Wealth of Nations: Principles of Economic Life* (New York: Random House, 1984).

47. Jacobs, *Death and Life*, 192.

48. Ibid., 198.

49. Talen, "Design That Enables Diversity," 234.

50. A. Duany, "Our Urbanism," *Architecture* 87, no. 12 (December 1998): 37–40.

51. A. Duany, "A Common Language of Urban Design," *Places* 11, no. 3 (1998): 76–78.

52. Duany, Plater-Zyberk, and Speck, *Suburban Nation*, 149.

53. A. Duany and E. Talen, "Making the Good Easy: The Smart Code Alternative," *Fordham Urban Law Journal* 29, no. 4 (2002): 1,445–68.

54. Kunstler, "Interview with Jane Jacobs."

55. B. Steigerwald, "Urban Studies Legend Jane Jacobs on Gentrification, the New Urbanism, and Her Legacy," *Reason.com* (June 2001); available at http://reason.com/archives/2001/06/01/city-views.

56. Ibid.

57. Kunstler, "Interview with Jane Jacobs."

58. J. L. Grant, "Theory and Practice in Planning the Suburbs: Challenges in Implementing New Urbanism and Smart Growth Principles," *Planning Theory and Practice* 10, no. 1 (2009): 11–33.

## PLANNING THE MODERN ARAB CITY: THE CASE OF ABU DHABI

1. Per www.government.ae/web/guest/geography, the latest figure is 8.19 million.

2. "Abu Dhabi in Figures 2010," Statistics centre – Abu Dhabi, p. 13; available at www.scad.ae/English/AD%20in%20figure%20ENGLISH%202010.pdf.

3. Abu Dhabi National Oil Company, "Energy & UAE"; available at www.adnoc.ae/content.aspx?newid=306&mid=306.

4. Abu Dhabi Statistical Office, Gross Domestic Product Report, 2008, p. 7; available at www.scad.ae/English/publications/Gross%20Domestic%20Product.pdf.

5. Abu Dhabi Statistical Office; see also World Bank, 2010, referenced at http://en.wikipedia.org/wiki/List_of_countries_by_GDP_(PPP)_per_capita.

6. "Abu Dhabi in Figures 2010," p. 26.

## JANE JACOBS, ANDY WARHOL, AND THE KIND OF PROBLEM A COMMUNITY IS

1. The paintings were not finished until 1962, but he began the series at this time. Neil Printz and Georg Frei, eds., *Andy Warhol Catalogue Raisonné*, vol. 1, *Paintings and Sculpture, 1961–1963* (New York: Phaidon Press, 2002), 64. I was the managing editor of this book.

2. For the context of these works as acts of participatory aesthetics, see Benjamin H. D. Buchloh, "Andy Warhol's One-Dimensional Art, 1956–1966," in *Andy Warhol*, ed. Annette Michelson (Cambridge, Mass.: MIT Press, 2001), 1–48.

3. The best overview of postwar urban renewal in New York City is Samuel Zipp, *Manhattan Projects: The Rise and Fall of Urban Renewal in Cold War New York* (New York: Oxford University Press, 2010).

4. One of the more revealing depictions of the evolving nature of urban community at this time was the ABC series *Naked City*, which ran from 1958 to 1963 and was notable for the extent to which it was shot on the streets of New York and ranged across the city's class strata.

5. As Georg Simmel noted in "The Metropolis and Mental Life" (1903), urban experience is inherently impersonal and defined by mechanisms of exchange that limit any one individual's exposure to others; it therefore cannot be encompassed by small-town social relations, if only for reasons of scale. Simmel's essay is included in *On Individuality and Social Forms*, ed. Donald N. Levine (Chicago: University of Chicago Press, 1971), 324–39.

6. Sennett's *The Uses of Disorder: Personal Identity and City Life* (New York: Alfred A. Knopf, 1970) remains a bracing depiction of the devolution of the concept of vibrant and diverse urban communities and its implications for contemporary cities. In Sennett's view, a strong urban community can exist only in an environment that is open about its internal divisions and conflicts and that does not even strive for orderliness.

7. Warhol was shot and severely wounded in 1968 by aspiring playwright Valerie Solanas, whose misandrist work he had declined to produce.

8. See, for example, Marco Livingstone, "Do It Yourself: Notes on Warhol's Techniques," in *Andy Warhol: A Retrospective*, ed. Kynaston McShine (New York: Museum of Modern Art, 1989), 63–78.

9. The story of Warhol, Moses, and the *Thirteen Most Wanted Men* mural is told in wonderful detail in chapter 3 of Richard Meyer, *Outlaw Representation: Censorship and Homosexuality in Twentieth-Century American Art* (New York: Oxford University Press, 2002).

10. My thanks to Colleen Frankhart, Robert Mennel, Edmund Morris, Max Page, Robert Perris, and Carolyn Torma for their comments on an earlier version of this essay.

## A CHINESE PERSPECTIVE

1. Liz Sidotti cites a Pew Research Center poll in "Trust in Government? Poll Finds Nearly 80% of Americans Don't," *Huffington Post* (April 19, 2010); available at www.huffingtonpost.com/2010/04/19/trust-in-government-poll_n_542423.html.

2. Zhengxu Wang, "Political Trust in China: Forms and Causes" (paper presented at the annual meeting of the Midwest Political Science Association, Chicago, April 18–22, 2004); available at www.allacademic.com//meta/p_mla_apa_research_citation/0/8/3/6/8/pages83684/p83684-3.php, 3.

3. See "China GDP Growth Rate," *Trading Economics*; available at www.tradingeconomics.com/Economics/GDP-Growth.aspx?Symbol=CNY.

4. Landholders only lease property in China, where the government owns all the land.

5. Michael Wines and Jonathan Ansfield, "Trampled in a Land Rush, Chinese Resist," *New York Times*, May 26, 2010; available at www.nytimes.com/2010/05/27/world/asia/27china.html.

## Jane Jacobs and the Death and Life of American Planning

1. For the record, it was not me who contributed "Trivial Profession."

2. Nathan Glazer, "Schools of the Minor Professions," *Minerva* 12, no. 3 (1974): 346–64.

3. F. Stuart Chapin Jr., *Urban Land Use Planning* (Champaign: University of Illinois Press, 1965), vi.

4. William Rich et al., "Holding Together: Four Years of Evolution at MIT," *Journal of the American Institute of Planners* 36, no. 4 (July 1970): 242–52.

5. I refer here to Mumford's long-winded critique of *Death and Life*: "Mother Jacobs' Home Remedies," *New Yorker*, December 1, 1962, 148–79.

6. Jane Jacobs, *The Death and Life of Great American Cities* (New York: Random House, 1961), 17–18. It is astonishing that Jacobs would fault Howard for being a planning amateur; she was, after all, herself a journalist with an equal lack of professional training in planning or design. Lewis Mumford was especially piqued at Jacobs's dismissal of Howard, his mentor and hero. See Mumford, "Mother Jacobs' Home Remedies."

7. Glazer, "Schools of the Minor Professions."

8. Rich et al., "Holding Together," 244.

9. Alex Krieger, "The Planner as Urban Designer: Reforming Planning Education," in *The Profession of City Planning: Changes, Images, and Challenges, 1950–2000*, ed. Lloyd Rodwin and Bishwapriya Sanyal (New Brunswick, N.J.: Center for Urban Policy Research / Rutgers University Press, 2000), 209.

10. Matthew J. Kiefer, "The Social Functions of NIMBYism," *Harvard Design Magazine* 28 (Spring/Summer 2008), 97.

11. Michael Malone et al., *27 Views of Hillsborough: A Southern Town in Prose and Poetry* (Hillsborough, N.C.: Eno Publishers, 2010), back cover.

12. See Ray Oldenburg, *The Great Good Place: Cafes, Coffee Shops, Community Centers, Beauty Parlors, General Stores, Bars, Hangouts and How They Get You Through the Day* (New York: Paragon House, 1989).

13. In no way do I mean this to be a criticism of our town planners, who are capable and well-trained professionals. But even the most gifted young professional has his or her hands tied by the institutional structure and professional strictures within which planning must operate in most American communities.

14. Jane Jacobs, "Are Planning Departments Useful?" *Ontario Planning Journal* 8, no. 4 (July/August 1993), 4–5. The speech and subsequent essay ignited a firestorm of debate among Canadian planners.

15. We need a three-year curriculum for the master's degree in planning. Landscape architecture, architecture, law, and business all long ago moved to this model. There is nothing aside from inertia stopping us from doing the same. The planning profession is an order of magnitude more complex than it was 50 years ago, and yet we still expect students to master it all in two years.

16. Jerold S. Kayden, "What's the Mission of Harvard's Planning Program?" *Harvard Design Magazine* 22 (Spring/Summer 2005), 4.

17. Rich et al., "Holding Together," 244.

18. "Department of City and Regional Planning," in *Record of the University of North Carolina at Chapel Hill*, no. 577 (Chapel Hill: University of North Carolina Press, 1967), 12, 19–21; "Department of City and Regional Planning," in *Record of the University of North Carolina at Chapel Hill*, no. 713 (Chapel Hill: University of North Carolina Press, 1967), 18–19.

19. Richard Dobbs, "Megacities," *Foreign Policy* (September/October 2010).

20. Vishaan Chakrabarti, "A Country of Cities," *Urban Omnibus*, July 2, 2009; available at http://urbanomnibus.net/2009/07/a-country-of-cities.

21. Fareed Zakaria, interview by Charlie Rose, *The Charlie Rose Show*, PBS, October 25, 2010.

22. Zakaria, *Charlie Rose Show*.

23. Vishaan Chakrabarti, "Being Dense About Denmark," UrbanOmnibus, December 16, 2009; available at http://urbanomnibus.net/2009/12/being-dense-about-denmark.

# CONTRIBUTORS

**Rudayna Abdo,** AICP, is director of planning at Otak International's Abu Dhabi office. She is the former director of the American Institute of Certified Planners at the American Planning Association and a former associate at Perkins+Will.

**Geoffrey M. Batzel,** AICP, is director of urban planning for KEO International Consultants. He holds a master's in business administration from the Kellogg School of Management and a master's in urban planning from McGill University.

**Thomas J. Campanella** is associate professor of urban planning and design at the University of North Carolina at Chapel Hill and currently a Fellow at the American Academy in Rome. He is a recipient of Guggenheim and Fulbright fellowships and has held teaching and visiting appointments at the Massachusetts Institute of Technology, Columbia University, the Harvard Graduate School of Design, Nanjing University, and the Chinese University of Hong Kong. Campanella's books include *The Concrete Dragon: China's Urban Revolution and What It Means for the World* (2008); *Republic of Shade: New England and the American Elm* (2003), winner of the Spiro Kostof Award; and *Cities from the Sky: An Aerial Portrait of America* (2001). He is also , with Lawrence Vale, of *The Resilient City: How Modern Cities Recover from Disaster* (2005).

**Nathan Cherry,** AICP, is vice president in charge of planning and urban design for the Los Angeles office of RTKL and author of *Grid / Street / Place: Essential Elements of Sustainable Urban Districts* (APA Planners Press, 2009).

**Jill L. Grant** is professor of planning at Dalhousie University. Her books include *Planning the Good Community: New Urbanism in Theory and Practice* (2006) and *The Drama of Democracy: Contention and Dispute in Community Planning* (1994).

**Richard Harris** is professor of geography and earth sciences at McMaster University. His books include *Creeping Conformity How Canada Became Suburban, 1900–1960* (2004) and *Unplanned Suburbs: Toronto's American Tragedy, 1900–1950* (1996).

**Gert-Jan Hospers** teaches economic geography at the University of Twente and has a special chair in city and regional marketing at the Radboud University Nijmegen, both in Netherlands. In 2004 he visited Jane Jacobs in Toronto. His writings on Jacobs have appeared in Dutch publications, as well as the *Canadian Journal of Regional Science, European Planning Studies*, and *Planning Theory and Practice*.

**Jane M. Jacobs** is professor of cultural geography at the University of Edinburgh School of GeoSciences. Her publications include (with R. Fincher) *Cities of Difference* (1998) and *Edge of Empire: Postcolonialism and the City* (1996).

**Sergio Kiernan** is the architecture editor of *Página 12*, the foremost investigative paper in Argentina, and the author of *Classical and Vernacular: The Architecture of Alejandro Moreno* and *SYASA 20 Years*, about the restoration of the Teatro Colon in Buenos Aires.

**Peter L. Laurence** is graduate director and assistant professor of architecture at the Clemson University School of Architecture. Parts of his dissertation, "Jane Jacobs, American Architectural Criticism and Urban Design

Theory, 1935–1965," have been published in the *Journal of Architectural Education*, the *Journal of the Society of Architectural Historians*, and the *Journal of Urban Design*.

**Timothy Mennel** is senior editor and acquisitions manager of Planners Press and PAS Reports at the American Planning Association in Chicago. He coedited *Green Community* (2009) and *Block by Block: Jane Jacobs and the Future of New York* (2007); his 2007 dissertation in geography was a three-volume annotated novel about Robert Moses. He has published in the *Journal of Planning History* and the *Journal of the Society of Architectural Historians* and has been an editor at the Andy Warhol Foundation for the Visual Arts, Random House, *Artforum*, and elsewhere.

**Max Page** is professor of architecture and history at the University of Massachusetts in Amherst. A 2003 Guggenheim Fellow, he teaches and writes about the design, development, and politics of cities and architecture. His most recent book is *The City's End: Two Centuries of Fantasies, Fears, and Premonitions of New York's Destruction* (2008), and he is the author of *The Creative Destruction of Manhattan, 1900–1940* (1999), which won the Spiro Kostof Award of the Society of Architectural Historians, for the best book on architecture and urbanism. He coedited *Building the Nation: Americans Write Their Architecture, Their Cities, and Their Environment* (2003), and *Giving Preserving a History: Histories of Historic Preservation in the United States* (2003). Page has written for *Architecture* magazine, the *New York Times*, *Metropolis*, the *Los Angeles Times*, and the *Boston Globe*. He is currently researching a book on the future of historic preservation, supported by a Fulbright Fellowship and a Howard Foundation Fellowship.

**Jamin Creed Rowan** is assistant professor of English at Brigham Young University. He specializes in U.S. literature since 1865, with a particular focus on urban literature and culture. His work has been supported by a grant from the Rockefeller Archive Center and has appeared in *American Literature* and *Studies in American Fiction*. His book *Urban Sympathy: The Death and Life of an American Intellectual Tradition* is forthcoming from the University of Pennsylvania Press.

# Index